My Life in the Welsh Guards

Sydney Pritchard

My Life in the Welsh Guards

1939-46

First edition: March 2007

© Copyright Sydney Pritchard and Y Lolfa Cyf., 2007

Cover design: Y Lolfa

ISBN-13: 978 0 86243 985 9
ISBN-10: 086243 985 X

Published and printed in Wales
by Y Lolfa Cyf., Talybont, Ceredigion SY24 5AP
website www.ylolfa.com
e-mail ylolfa@ylolfa.com
tel. 01970 832 304
fax 832 782

F RIDAY, 29TH DECEMBER 1939. I left my home at Godreaman, Aberdare to catch the 10.30 am train at Aberaman station, accompanied by my parents. They were seeing me off on the first stage of my journey, to join the Welsh Guards at their depot in Caterham, Surrey.

Arriving in Paddington during the blackout, with no experience of the tube system, was quite bewildering for a young lad who had never been away from home. Somehow, I eventually reached my destination, and was looking forward to serving in the army. My joy was somewhat diminished when supper arrived, consisting of cheese, onion and chunks of bread, something I never ate at home. Bedtime was an even bigger shock as I had to sleep on the bare floorboards, with just one blanket.

The following day saw us new recruits being fitted out with uniforms, which consisted of one battledress, one service dress, denim trousers and blouse for general fatigues, underwear, cap, badge and one grey great coat. To this was added a pair of boots, which had to be highly polished by Monday morning, ready for a general inspection, which meant Sunday was spent burning and boning, unofficially, for a brilliant shine.

This method was quicker than polishing but could damage the boots. Also, at this point, we were issued with our army numbers; mine was 2735347.

For the next four weeks we were confined to barracks for intensive training. One of the biggest parts of this training was learning to walk and march in the manner expected of a guardsman. During this time, guardsmen Jeffers, Thornley and I were chosen out of our section of twenty-one to be promoted to section leaders, the first step on the promotion ladder. At the end of the four weeks, we passed out, and were allowed to leave the depot during our free time, which was very limited. Two more weeks found me and seven others doing our first guard duties outside the barracks.

In all, we had eight weeks of training at Caterham, after which we were taken to Romanway camp, Colchester. This was for around three weeks of intensive outdoor training with the training battalion. It was only after all this that were we allowed our first seven-day break, which saw me heading for home and all the comforts I had missed.

April saw us back in camp, continuing with our training. This time, we were split into groups, some for the British Expeditionary Force in France and others to London, before being posted on.

I was sent to the Tower of London for a stay of just a few hours, before joining the 2nd Battalion Welsh Guards at Olddean Common, Camberley in Surrey. Here we slept under canvas for some weeks, during which time we had intensive training, day and night.

Around the 11th May, we were given a week's leave, so I headed home for Aberdare. Unfortunately, Hitler and Germany had other ideas and began the Blitzkrieg on the Western Front. All leave was cancelled, but I had got as far as Cardiff when I heard (I was actually on the Aberdare train). I fully intended to go back (honestly). I went back to the London line and I met some others, who said, "They've some bloody hope; we're going home," and so we hid in the lavatory all the way from Cardiff to Bridgend. My friend went home to Swansea, another boy went to the Rhondda and I went to Aberdare. When we got back to Olddean Common, it was deserted, and we were taken to the guardroom and asked why we had not come back. We said we never had a telegram. Then the boys came back.

After breakfast on Tuesday morning, the 21st May 1940, we were ordered to assemble our fighting kit together, as we were leaving for an unknown destination. Once our journey had begun, we were informed that our destination was Dover. During our journey, we were issued with 50 rounds of rifle ammunition, with a briefing to kill, sabotage and destroy. At this point, it was reiterated that we were completely on our own and that we were not to expect any further assistance from anyone. We were also informed that we would only be encountering plywood German tanks. This made it obvious to us that our destination would be France.

On our arrival at the harbour (name unknown), night had already fallen. We had to make our way carefully, scrambling over the sleeping bodies of civilians and soldiers (the latter having escaped from France).

We boarded a Royal Navy frigate. I believe it was called either *Queen of the Channel* or *Biarritz,* and this took us over the Channel to land at Boulogne, by which time it was daylight. The journey had taken slightly longer than it should have done, due to the fact that we had been chased several times by U-boats.

Our Company (No. 4) was the last to disembark. During the unloading operation, we received our first two casualties, one of whom was a trained machine-gunner. This loss meant that Sergeant Henry and I were responsible for caring for the machine gun and tripod, together with our own rifles. We were then ordered to march through the town of Boulogne, where I had the misfortune to trip and fall, loaded with the tripod and my rifle. This caused me to twist my knee badly, which meant I had to limp the next few miles uphill to the village of St Martins, overlooking Boulogne.

On our arrival, we were ordered to dig in and construct road blocks. We were aware that a German spotter plane had already seen us, as well as a sniper in the church tower.

Due to the casualties already sustained, I was asked to man the anti-tank rifle on my own for two hours. I had never seen one before, let alone fired one. On top of this, I had only been issued with three rounds of ammunition. To say I was not happy with the situation was an understatement. When the end of my shift came, I was extremely relieved.

By dusk that day, everyone was in position and a night patrol was organised for reconnaissance. This party consisted of an officer, a sergeant and two guardsmen, of whom I was one. Our password was 'The Tower', being the home of the battalion whilst in London. Having ventured several hundred yards away, we encountered a French family and others in our tracks. Luckily, our Officer, Captain Cwm Tennant, spoke fluent French and he gathered some useful information on the whereabouts of the enemy. The French family accompanied us back through our lines to safety.

That tour of duty completed, I was ordered to stand down and grab some sleep, and so, after reporting my whereabouts to my sergeant, I gratefully did as ordered, under the nearest hedgerow.

Just before daybreak on the Thursday morning, I was aroused from sleep by my sergeant and ordered to stand to immediately. Later, I was ordered to stand down for a wash and to freshen up. En route to the water pump, a few hundred yards away, I knocked on the door of a cottage, to ask the lady of the house to warm a tin of soup (this had been issued during the night). Much to my horror and surprise, she slammed the door in my face. Stunned, I carried on to the water pump to wash, when, to my even greater horror, the enemy opened fire on me. We had obviously been spotted the day before by the spotter plane. I quickly gathered my gear together and, rounding up the other five guardsmen, who were in my charge, entered one of the cottages as a temporary shelter, so that I could assess our position.

The sergeant then arrived with new orders. Unknown to me, a decision had been made by my commanding officer, Major Higgins, second-in-command, Captain Cwm Tennant and the sergeant that I was to be made an acting NCO and to be placed in charge of the remainder of the section. I had made a great impression on the officers, both here and in London, with my behaviour and attitude. This order was to stay in force until our return to England, when I would be promoted officially to NCO.

Assessing that our situation was getting beyond our control, it was decided to try to contact headquarters for further instructions; the answer we received was not good. We were told, "The last man, the last round." With our position getting more precarious, the sergeant and I decided that we had to get away; we instructed the men on the direction to town, then gave the order, "Every man for himself." The sergeant and I waited until all the men had gone, then we made our own retreat.

During this retreat, the sergeant and I found a wounded comrade, who had an arm injury, lying by the roadside. On closer inspection, we found him to be Sergeant Sankey. Supporting him to the best of our ability, we travelled cautiously to the edge of the town. After assessing the safety of the town, we handed the injured sergeant Sankey over to the RAMC and made our way to the large mansion serving as our headquarters. When we arrived, we were informed that a small contingent of Welsh Guards had appeared, just before us. These turned out to be our men that we had sent on earlier, so we found them and re-organised ourselves. We were then sent to observe the enemy from a distance (I was posted under a privet hedge, which was most uncomfortable), to report any advancement of the enemy's armour. With no movement detected, we were recalled to the centre of the town. We had to take great precautions as the town was now partly occupied by fifth columnists, and there was the added danger of sniper fire. Orders filtered through to congregate in the fish market for further instructions, but our journey took longer than anticipated, owing to the enemy sniper fire. The sergeant and I managed to stay together, taking turns to cover one another so that we could cross roads and gaps safely. I was following the sergeant, at a reasonable distance and in sight of our destination, when we were spotted by the enemy. In my haste, I fell over some bodies; the sergeant quickly doubled back and dragged me the last few yards into the small entrance of the fish market, saving my life.

In the market, we met up with other guardsmen and were briefed about the current situation. We were all to make our way to the dockside, where the Royal Navy was to be waiting to evacuate us back to England. It was decided to make the short journey in small groups as there were lots of open spaces and a bridge to cross. This was to be blown up after the last man had crossed. My trip was uneventful, but the sight that met my eyes on arrival at the quayside was amazing. There were hundreds of officers and men already there, and waiting for the boats to return us to England.

We were formed into battalions, and with headquarters number 1 Company, the remainders were 2, 3 and 4, we proceeded to embark. Another attempt to eat a tin of soup, after puncturing it with my bayonet, failed when we got the orders to move on as the boat had arrived.

The wounded men were loaded first, irrespective of rank. Being near at hand, I assisted with a stretcher case as it was going on board. Getting near the top of the gangway and about to board the ship, a fellow guardsman (who informed me he was a married man) asked me if he could take over. This I let him do, and I returned to my company's position at the end of the queue. The ship managed to leave, after instructions had been left, telling us it would be back after dark to pick us up.

Everything had been going like clockwork, when suddenly, from nowhere, German aircraft appeared and started bombing and machine-gunning the quay. After diving for what cover we could find, we had to stay low until the air raid was over. Then, we had to re-organise ourselves and prepare to settle down, to wait for the next arrival of the Royal Navy.

Much to everyone's surprise, we were informed that, for safety reasons, it would be advisable for us to move from the quay. We were told to make for a point about 10–15 kilometres down the coast. It was nearly nightfall by the time we had formed up, with HQ at the front and 4 Company to bring up the rear.

Marching in an orderly manner and not having eaten since breakfast on Tuesday, 21st May, we were in no mood for laughter, so the order to march quietly and remain silent seemed a bit redundant.

We cautiously proceeded back to Boulogne, where we were taken down narrow side streets. A sudden burst of machine gun fire came from the direction in which we were marching. The leading companies were mown down, with no chance to shelter or to defend themselves. Fortunately, being with No 4 Company, we were at the rear of the line and I was quickly able to take shelter in a doorway until things had quietened down.

Eventually, the few of us left regrouped and made our way back towards the town. We met a non-commissioned officer, who was known to some of the others. He advised us to hide in a coal cellar in a nearby hotel for a few hours.

By a strange coincidence, there beside me was my old squad mate, Bert Jeffers. Between ourselves, we decided we would take a chance and make our way back to the jetty, on our own; and so, early on the Friday morning, 24th May, although it was a suicidal decision, we proceeded cautiously, making use of all the available cover. We managed to reach the jetty just before daybreak and, luckily, there was a mist over the harbour, giving us some cover.

Much to our great amazement, Major Windsor Lewis and a small number of guardsmen were already there. The Major made a decision to get as near as possible to the end of the jetty, with the possibility of being picked by the Royal Navy. As it was too dangerous to venture out in large numbers, it was decided that an NCO and two guardsmen would attempt to crawl forward as far as possible, to make a reconnaissance of the situation. The Major wanted volunteers, preferably single men. Corporal Jones (a North Walian), Jeffers (also known as Jeff) and I stepped forward. We were then briefed on our duties, and it was decided that one man would return, to give an account of what was ahead. Corporal Jones was in the lead, then Jeff and I at a reasonable distance behind. After all our care, we were very surprised when we came across some French civilians sheltering on the jetty. Also, a return journey was not necessary, as the remaining guardsmen were right behind us. They had been forced to follow on almost immediately, due to very heavy enemy gunfire directly on to the black shed they had been sheltering in. Our new position was very exposed and we were fully occupied trying to conceal ourselves, as we were in direct line of fire from enemy tanks and small arms fire.

Scattered along the jetty were abandoned Red Cross carriages, which proved highly useful in concealing us, but, unfortunately, we were still taking heavy casualties. Even though darkness was falling, there was still a small hope that we would be rescued by the Navy. All the remaining guardsmen were assembled in one small area. This meant that we could move quickly if needed. We all tried to get a little bit of sleep and were just desperately hoping the situation would improve by morning.

With dawn breaking on the Saturday morning, any hopes of now being rescued were greatly diminished. There was great concern for all the wounded men, as food, water, medical supplies and ammunition were now in short supply.

Major Lewis decided to brief us on our next moves, as we were still having casualties. These casualties were worrying, as they were happening and no one could explain them. It was decided to position three men, instead of two, at our observation posts, in the hope something would be spotted. Finally, the mystery was solved: a fifth columnist had infiltrated our ranks, dressed as one of us. He had been going around shooting our men in the back of their heads. When he had been captured, Major Lewis gave the order to execute him and throw him into the sea.

When we reached mid morning, it was the turn of

guardsmen Rees, Jeffers and me to take our turn on duty at the dangerous position at the end of the jetty. This was the suicide position, as any advancement from the enemy meant that we would be the first target. Due to this danger, the duty time was only one hour. Midway through our duty, Guardsman Rees was wounded in his left arm. A decision was made that, when conditions allowed, we would get back, to take up another position, under cover of the harbour.

Around midday, Major Lewis received an ultimatum to surrender by half-past two, or be completely wiped out by heavy tank fire. We were by this time down to thirteen Welsh guardsmen who were uninjured, the remainder were all wounded.

After much consultation, taking into account that we had with us a number of women and children, French soldiers and a few remnants from other regiments of the British Expeditionary Force, it was decided by the Major to surrender after a given time.

The Major, at this point, took note of Corporal Jones, Jeffers and my names; this was for further recognition. The citation was to read: "For crawling out, in the direct face of the enemy, for the benefit of all the others, to seek more shelter." The Major then ordered us to destroy all our personal belongings and weapons. At the agreed time, a high ranking German officer, with others, marched in on us.

The German officer was astonished at how so few men had held out for so long, and although he had been wounded in the face, he congratulated us on such a heroic fight. Then, speaking fluent English, the officer informed us that, by Christmas, the

Germans would be in London and feasting at Buckingham Palace, and that for us the war was now over. We were then searched, but, unknown to them, I had hidden my cap badge in my sock. Luckily, they failed to find it.

Concerned about our wounded, we were allowed, with help from our captors, to make them as comfortable as possible, before being marched off. We were taken from the jetty towards town. On our way, we spotted a person in a British uniform being driven in a German staff car. We were all of the opinion that this was a second fifth columnist, who had also infiltrated our ranks, causing the loss of more of our boys, especially those who had been in impregnable positions.

Reaching the town of Boulogne, the Welsh Guardsmen were separated from the rest and were taken to a back alley court-yard. When we were able to talk, we all confessed that we had said a small prayer, as we thought our lives were going to be ended.

After about an hour, we were marched out to join the remnants of other regiments. We were then paraded around the town of Boulogne, which had, in the space of a few hours, changed beyond recognition. Houses we had been defending with our lives were now flying the Swastika flag of Hitler. We then marched out through the village of St Martin, where we had been positioned only days earlier. Here, we marched past the basic wooden crosses on the graves of our fallen comrades, with whom we had served.

At nightfall, we were ushered into a local sports field. Our numbers had been increased by more prisoners en route. After the heat wave we had experienced for the last few days, the heavens opened. There was a huge thunderstorm and torrential rain. With no protection, the most we could do was huddle together and keep each other company.

On the Sunday morning, 26th May, at the crack of dawn, we returned to the open road. Our destination was unknown to us and we were told that anyone attempting to escape would be shot immediately, along with a number of other soldiers.

We were now in a position to see at first hand the enormous preparations made by the Germans in anticipation of crossing the Channel. There were sections of portable bridges attached to their tanks and mobile units. All the things we had been told were made of cardboard and hardboard were now in front of us, as solid and real as ourselves. Along with the heavy armour, there were miles and miles of supporting equipment. The Germans were full of confidence, expecting to be in England in a couple of weeks and the war to be over.

This march was to last fourteen days, taking us from Boulogne to Belgium in the sweltering heat. If we were lucky enough to pass through villages, then some kind folk would place buckets of water and sometimes food at the wayside for us. However, to the obvious delight of the German guards, the guards would kick over the water pails and watch us as the water trickled away. As we were marching, around ten days after leaving Britain, and not having eaten since then, it was decided between another soldier, Findas, Jeffers and myself that one of us would risk breaking rank at the first opportunity, to search for food. This fell on my shoulders as I drew the short straw. For some reason, the column was halted in a small village and, by some good fortune, we were outside a house with an open door. Making a quick decision to take a chance and enter, to beg or steal something to eat, the other two wished me the best of luck, and off I went.

Much to my amazement, the first room I entered contained a four poster bed and propped up against the pillows, in a little white bonnet and shawl, was this little old lady. So, in my broken French, I asked for any bread, eggs or something to eat, but there was no response. That is when I realized that the old lady was dead. Owing to the circumstances and my own conscience, I left everything alone and I retraced my steps empty-handed. Unfortunately, I was met in the doorway by a German guard, and I immediately thought that my number was up, as did the others, but instead, he took a running kick at me with his jack boots, making contact with my back as I made a getaway. Much to the amazement of my two mates, I was still alive to march on, although still hungry. One consolation was that I had had my attempt and it now fell on one of the others to do the next. I remembered something my father had told me many times. If you are ever without water, suck two small pebbles to produce saliva in your mouth. This is what we did, and it helped us enormously.

Around this time, towards evening, we were turned out into a huge field, where other prisoners had congregated. We were even more amazed when we heard there was the likelihood of something to eat. This was being cooked in one corner, where they were slaughtering cattle and boiling the carcass for distribution among us as so called soup. This was thankfully received, even after queuing for hours, and our ration was put into steel helmets that we had picked up on our march.

Having marched roughly five days by this time, the three of us had learnt that, to receive any help from the French locals, for scraps of food, you had to march as near to the front of the column as possible, although there was a certain limit and great risk of being machine gunned down, should any trouble arise. As the number of prisoners was now in the hundreds, we were surrounded by trigger-happy German guards behind machine guns and Bren guns.

A few days later, it fell on Jeffers's shoulders to take his attempt at getting food. This meant that as we were passing a field, he had to dive in to see what he could grab. In this field, clamps of potato were stored, and to our good fortune, Jeffers got away without being seen. This resulted in us having a few raw potatoes and bruised onions (I still loathe the sight and smell of them) to eat.

Coming to the end of the first week, I was more than surprised to hear my name being called and then being slapped on the back. Looking round, I came face to face with a boy, Jim, who lived right opposite my home in Aberdare, which proved a great asset to me later. He had been in France for some months, therefore was very familiar with the language. Back home, my parents had been very kind to him and his family, by supplying them with fresh vegetables and other things during the depression. He produced two eggs from his pocket, which I had to swallow immediately. We agreed to look for each other every day. My only regret was not being able to share my good fortune with Bert Jeffers and another guardsman, Genders. It was decided that the next food we received would be shared between those two and not me. As arranged, Jim and I had the good fortune to meet the next day; this time, he had one egg, which he gave to me, for which he apologised. Jim noticed that I was limping and so he enquired what was wrong. I explained to him that my feet were swollen so much that my boots were too tight. He immediately suggested that, on the next stop, we should exchange boots (as he took a larger size) for which I was most grateful, although mine had been highly polished and his were smothered in dubbin.

We were marched approximately twenty miles a day. On or around the tenth day of our march, officially still not having had anything to eat or drink from our captors, and sleeping in the open every night, fortunately the weather was dry but very warm. The old proverb: 'British Army marches on its stomach' was one hundred percent right. It was around this time that we learnt that a number of British Prisoners of War had been put into barns, and then machine gunned and the buildings set alight. Obviously, this horrified us as we did not know if the same fate awaited us.

On crossing the Maginot line, we were invited by our captors to, "Hang out our Washing on the Siegfried Line," which was a popular tune at the time. We ignored their kind invitation. However, we would have appreciated some food or drink, but it was not to be.

When we halted for the night, it was by the side of a small canal, which gave us the opportunity to have a wash down, as we had not had a proper wash since being captured. Somehow, Jeff produced his own razor and blade, so we then endeavoured to scrape off ten days of growth, which was a welcome relief.

By now, it appeared that we were on the borders of

Belgium. It was here that we observed a dog drawing a milk churn on a little cart. It was Saturday and fourteen days after our capture. We were turned into a field, hungry, thirsty and exhausted. There we remained until midday on the Sunday, when we again returned to the road. Having marched only a few miles, we were surprised to be turned into a railway siding. After a short wait, convoys of cattle trucks were shunted into the sidings and we were ordered to line up in fours. We were instructed that, if there was any attempt to escape, then we would be shot on sight. Gradually, the column was boarded onto these wagons, roughly about fifty to sixty men to each truck. Before entering the trucks, and much to our delight and astonishment, we were given one loaf of bread between four. Although gratefully received, we had to be careful of the mildew. You had to be sure of who you were sharing with, but, luckily, there were three of us friends, so we only needed one other person to share with us. Once inside the wagon, we divided the bread equally, not an easy task under the circumstances, also we did not want to waste one little crumb. When the right number of men were all in, the door was slammed closed and firmly bolted, leaving us like cattle, with only two small vents for air and even this was wired off to prevent escape.

Although the conditions were bad, we were pretty thankful, as we were now being carried instead of being marched.

There we remained until nightfall, when we eventually began to move towards a destination as yet unknown. The overcrowded conditions did not allow everyone to sit down, so it was up to each individual to arrange who stood and who sat. The people standing would be supporting each other in the best way possible, not an easy task whilst the train was being shunted. Jeffers, Genders and I had an arrangement for standing and sitting in equal measure. Before the end of twenty-four hours, tempers were getting very short, especially as toilet facilities were not provided and the only alternative was to relieve yourself where you stood. Urinating was no problem, but the stench eventually went beyond what a human could stand. Luckily, our natural bodily functions, apart from urinating, were nil, as we had not really eaten anything since our last breakfast in England.

Tuesday afternoon, approximately forty-eight hours after being put onto the cattle trucks, the sun and heat became suffocating and the trucks were still being shunted to and fro. During one of our siding stops, we heard the yelling and screaming of our guards. Eventually, we heard our doors being unlocked and opened, and, to our surprise, a bucket of water was placed in the doorway. We assumed it was to be shared between all of us, but, human nature being what it is, those who were nearest went to help themselves. Unfortunately, owing to the stampede, the bucket was overturned; consequently, we were again without water. The only thing we gained was a further short breath of fresh air as the door was immediately opened for the empty bucket to be removed. The German guards were then heard in chorus, laughing and singing, "Mad Englishmen".

During the hours of darkness, for some unknown reason, I searched through my pockets and was thrilled to find, dirty and sticky, four Rowntree's fruit gums. These were the remains of a food parcel which I had received whilst under canvas in England. The flavours were immaterial to us and so much appreciated by the three of us. The last one was saved for sucking later.

Around the third day of travelling, we were shunted into sidings and one of the lads recognised it as Berlin. After a few hours, we were again on the move, travelling throughout the night and well into the next day. When we next stopped, the doors were opened and, much to our relief, we were allowed to get out of the train and onto the railway sidings. Obviously, they made sure that we would not do anything stupid, by announcing through a loudspeaker that, for anyone who tried to escape, they would take twenty prisoners to one side and shoot them. With all the suffering and humiliation we had suffered, common sense prevailed and no one attempted to escape. Anyway, we were only too grateful that we were at last able to stretch our legs and breathe fresh air, after being cramped up for so long. Also, no one had the strength or the ability to attempt to run away. Unfortunately, this small amount of freedom was not to last long and we were once again herded back onto the cattle trucks.

Another day dawned, with tempers and conditions still no better, still cramped and baking hot. We travelled through the day, with no food and unable to sleep, and as darkness fell, we prepared for another long night. About midnight, we came to an abrupt halt. With bright arc lights shining all around, we were shunted into the sidings. We heard loud shouting and the opening of doors. We were ordered to get out, some falling out and others rolling out, through exhaustion. Facing us were heavily armed Germans, and we were given strict orders to line up in fives ready for counting. Those who were unable to get up were hastily assisted by a jack boot or a rifle. Eventually, we were marched away from the railway sidings and along a cobbled road, passing a high wall surrounded by rows and rows of barbed wire and huge floodlights scanning the area. This was obviously new and a POW camp. Information trickled through from someone that we were in Poland. Passing the heavy iron doors, we were made to march for another forty-five minutes. Then, we came face to face with another heavily wired fortification. This was to be our destination. Once again, we were ordered to form up in lines of five and then we were marched into a huge military compound.

We were met by a senior British NCO (non commissioned officer) who marched us over the drawbridge and detailed us off to different areas, in groups of thirty. We were taken to a barrack room and told that this was our living quarters. Jeffers and I reserved a space for ourselves down the centre of the room. Although on bare boards, we were only too grateful to be able to undress, remove our boots and stretch out for a few hours sleep, for the first time since our long and tedious march through France, and the deplorable conditions endured for five days and nights on the cattle trucks.

After what seemed like only a few minutes, we were aroused by the yelling and screeching of the German guards. We were ordered, by fair means or foul, to get up and dressed for counting, and, due to the deprivation, hardship and starvation of the past weeks, we quickly obeyed. We were given a small issue of German so-called coffee. This was very gratefully received by all.

During the course of the day, we met up with other British prisoners and were enlightened as to our whereabouts and camp procedure. Apparently, we were in the town of Thorn, in the Polish Corridor, and our new home was an old military fortress, surrounded by a moat, which had been drained dry, affording us more walking space. Throughout the day, we had been cautioned about the dos and don'ts of the camp, which was Stalag XXA11.

At around midday, we were given a token and instructed to line up to receive a small quantity of watery turnip soup from the cook house. Having devoured this, we again reminisced about our times back home, and elsewhere, when we had refused appetising meals, such as Sunday roast and cream teas. The next meal we had was the bread that was issued at about four o'clock, which consisted of a one kilo loaf between five men, a spoonful of so-called jam, or a small portion of margarine, sufficient for one slice only. Although the brown bread looked and tasted like sawdust, it was heartily eaten, with not a crumb wasted. The biggest problem with it was that it was a twenty-four hour ration, and that I had to cut and share the loaf into five equal pieces, with four pairs of hungry eyes watching to ensure that I did not cut one portion bigger than the others. With no knife, I made do with half a brass button-stick, which we had found.

In the next few days, we were detailed to various jobs inside and outside the camp compound. I vividly remember my first glimpse of the outside surroundings. This was when I was marched to a sand pit, to start loading sand. This was heavy work, especially on such meagre rations. Late in the afternoon, we returned to camp, having silently and regularly thanked God for helping us to survive another day.

Much to our relief, a few days later, we were taken from room to room, to the moat outside. We were to be formally registered as British Prisoners of War. This immediately made us feel safer, and our families would at least know that we were alive. We were individually marched up to a table, where we were asked our name, number, nationality and home address. We were given our POW number; mine was THORN, STALAG XXA 6340. I was given a disc, which was in two parts; this was always to be carried round my neck. Then a photograph was taken of our head and shoulders. I was registered as a blonde, although, when I left Blighty, my hair was dark brown. During the march through France, my hair had been bleached by the rays of the sun. Thinking ahead, I registered as a cobbler, although I had never repaired a shoe in my life. Jeffers registered as a hairdresser, and Genders as a butcher, with the sole intention of staying together, which proved unsuccessful. Somehow, I still have a photostat copy of the original registration.

This registration all took place in mid June 1940. During the next 10–14 days, life continued in the same way, apart from being issued with the Red Cross postcards to send home, with strict instructions on what we should write. Needless to say, the things we required soon filled our postcards, not for one moment imagining that they would get to their destinations (however, on this we were proved wrong).

Towards the end of June (now in a daily routine of work),

I was in a working party that was breaking stones to use for laying roads (having left Jeffers and Genders as usual), when I heard my number being called by an excited German guard. I stood up from my crouching position, to acknowledge his call, and I had to display my numbered disc, to prove who I was. To everyone's amazement, I was immediately marched off at double quick time, having no idea what I had done to deserve this. Eventually, I arrived at the German headquarters, where all the information on British POWs was kept. Also stored here were all the confiscated uniforms etc. I was marched to the clothing store, where I was given a blanket, a pair of wooden Dutch clogs (2-3 sizes too big), two foot cloths, a water bottle, a dixie can and a huge French cavalry coat. This I took as a great insult to my pride and, on leaving the storeroom, I saw a British single breasted great coat hanging up. The temptation was too great, so I exchanged them, feeling much happier with my new coat. Last but not least, I was given half a loaf of bread, which was to last me for the next two days.

Finally, I was told that I was being marched approximately two miles, to Thorn railway station. When I got there, I was joined by a group of nineteen fellow POWs. We were then herded into a civilian compartment, amongst Polish travellers. This was a luxury in itself, after the last journey by cattle truck. We eventually arrived in the Polish town of Bromberg, where we were treated to an amazing welcome from the Polish people, as we were the first British prisoners they had seen. As we were marching from the station, we were showered with flowers, miniature rolls of bread and a variety of other foods, much to the annoyance of the Germans, who were shouting and bawling. Needless to say, we collected as much as possible, for a future feast. We were then put on a miniature railway, to travel inland for about an hour, arriving in the heart of the countryside. We disembarked at a little village halt, and were marched a few kilometres down the road. We reached our destination, which was a medium sized mansion, probably a house that had belonged to a member of the Polish gentry. Attached to the house were a farm and some small cottages. We were taken into the mansion, which, to our surprise, was to be our new home, although we did have to share it with our armed German guard, and the open spaces, inside as well as outside, were separated with barbed wire.

There was a mad scramble upstairs, to get the best places to sleep out of the three allocated bedrooms. I was fortunate to allocate myself a corner position. Later on, we had to reassemble in the compound for counting and briefing, and we noticed an old army field kitchen, which was to be for our use. We were then told why we had been brought here. Our sole purpose was to take down all the barbed wire entanglements that had been used by the Polish army to delay advancing Germans throughout the area. This was to be restored and sent back to Germany for further use. Before being dismissed, my number was called out, along with another, and we were told that we were going to be the shoe repairer and tailor for the camp. We were both taken outside the wire compound, to the rooms below ground level in the mansion, where I was shown and given the tools required to do repairs. After the shock of seeing the tools I was to use, I regretted very much having registered as a shoe repairer. The tools consisted of a foot last fixed into a length of wood, which was to be held between the knees, a hammer, pincers, a bradawl with a box of wooden pegs, a quantity of split leg hob nails, a sack full of leather off cuts for repairing soles and uppers, a roll of twine and cobblers wax. For someone who had only been an onlooker at a shoe repairers, I was completely lost on where and how to start when the time came. The tailor was a little, cockney, Jewish boy and, like myself, I felt that he, too, did not have the experience of tailoring expected of him. His tools were also limited and outdated for the job.

When we started work, it appeared that the work we were to do was the same as everyone else, which was to cut down the barbed wire entanglements, which had been put up by the Poles to delay the advance of the enemy. As time progressed, this was causing a lot of injuries to our hands and limbs, as they were constantly being torn by the wire, and we were not provided with any protection whatsoever.

Eventually, I was called upon to re-stud some of the lads' boots, therefore I was confined to camp, which I was very pleased about. The alternative was being knee deep in swamps. I was quite surprised, when I was also given the guards' heavy duty jack boots and told to replace the lead tip and studs. This was encouraging, as it meant that my work was satisfactory but also I would be given a hunk of bread or a piece of sausage extra to normal rations. These I shared with the tailor boy, and he would do likewise.

Our work room was below ground and part of the old kitchen quarters for the pre-war mansion, where all the food was prepared. This was still being used once or twice a week, for baking purposes, by the Polish people who still occupied the home farm. This eventually proved to be to our advantage in more ways than one. Each morning and evening, a pail of milk would be brought over from the farm and put into cold storage, officially for the use of the guards. Unknown to them, the tailor and I would have our fill and then replace what we had drunk with water to the level it was before. We dare not take any away for the others, as our 'helpings' would be discovered.

Baking days were the highlight of our week and very much looked forward to, as the Polish servant would pass us some bread. This was a great risk for her as her life was in danger if she was caught assisting us.

After approximately four to five weeks, the removal of the barbed wire was now taking place much further afield. Once more, we were on the move, this time our sleeping quarters were two rooms in a village school. We had all been issued with huge wooden clogs, which were to be worn instead of our boots. Although the repairing of boots had eased, I had another task placed upon me. Having first aid knowledge, I was called upon every day to treat fellow comrades for blisters and very sore feet. The worst job was dealing with the festering wounds caused by the barbed wire scratches. My only tools for this job were a razor blade and sunshine. The first was to release the pus, and the latter to dry the wound.

Towards the end of July, we were given a Saturday off. Not for us, but because we were being visited by high ranking German officers. Therefore, we had to be as clean as possible, quite a bit of a problem, as we were without washing facilities.

Although we had already lost our heads of hair, we were ordered to spruce up the little growth we had grown since being cropped just a few weeks previously.

On the day of their arrival, my name was called out with two others, and I was taken away into the guards' quarters, which were in an old house that had belonged to gentry. Having been taken indoors, we were put into a well furnished room. The two others were called away separately, leaving me on my own. After what seemed like an absolute age, with no sign of the other two, I was eventually called and taken under escort by two immaculate German officers into a room. Laid out in front of me was a table full of wine, food and fruit of every description. Sat around the table were other high ranking German officers, in all their splendour. I was taken to sit down at the centre of the table and was greatly tempted to snatch away some of the luxury facing me. Eventually, my name, rank etc. were read out to me, which I confirmed as correct. In perfect English, I was then ordered to answer the following questions. Was I a Welshman? Did my family live in Wales? Where in Wales did they live? Why was I in the British army (being a Welshman)? And why did I fight for England, being a Welshman? Now the penny began to drop, especially with all the luxuries laid out in front of me. For comfort, good living quarters and a limited amount of freedom, they wanted my cooperation, to wear a German uniform and join their ranks. They also wanted me to do radio broadcasting and non combat fighting. Without any hesitation on my part, my reply was a firm NO! They insisted, however, that I took more time to think about all the things I would be missing for the duration of the war and afterwards. Although I had been given some more time to reconsider my decision, and having been pampered with a few more luxuries, I still stuck to my original refusal. I was then taken under escort back to camp. Fearing a reprisal at a future date proved to be correct; in a matter of days, whilst sitting outside in the camp enclosure, having my short growth of hair trimmed, my camp friend was ordered to remove all my hair again, which made me extra cautious of all my daily movements.

Luckily, it was my good fortune that, just three weeks after this incident, we were no longer required to carry on with the further removal of the barbed wire. We were returned to the main camps in Thorn.

It was now early September 1940, and I was in Stalag XXA17, which was right opposite the city's main railway station. From here, I went out daily on various jobs, the main one was working in the stables, amongst the horses which had been used by the Polish Cavalry. Here, we were able to pick up a little extra bread and other bits from the Polish civilians, although they were under strict instructions from the SS not to communicate with us. We had to work alongside serving German soldiers, young men like ourselves. Some were favourable, others were not, but it gave us the opportunity to pick up a little of their language.

Although working in the stables meant long hours and hard work, it took us out of the large camp environment. The camp could be very depressing, seeing fit young British soldiers letting themselves deteriorate from hunger and boredom. The only highlight was that, during the evening count, a small quantity of mail was being received from England. Unfortunately, my name was not called out, but after the contents were shared amongst us, some were humorous, others contained tragic news. One of our favourite topics, which caused much laughter and got increasingly popular as the years went by, was how many wives and girlfriends 'found' strange babies on their doorsteps.

Around this time, I remember that I was on a working party along with others at a flour mill, and under the supervision of a Prussian civilian. It was obvious for more reasons than one that he hated the British Tommy and did all in his power to try to shoot us on the spot. He had to make do with using us for slave labour, to carry full sacks of flour into the railway wagons destined for Germany, but, unknown to him, and when the opportunity arose, we would burst open the sacks and urinate into the flour. We hoped that this meant that, when the flour reached its destination, much would be ruined. To be on this particular working party was a nightmare, as we were constantly harassed and butted by the guards, and to collapse would have been fatal, as this meant that you would receive rifle butts and savage kicks from them. This was one working party that everyone wished hard to avoid in the mornings, and although this was only half a day, it was a blessing to return to camp, stretch out and relax on the bare boards and thank God for letting us survive another day.

This camp was under the charge of CSM Hamer of the Rifle Brigade, who was captured in Calais on the 26th May 1940, whilst carrying out standing duties by controlling approximately five hundred ill-tempered and hungry men.

After roll call each night, he made us sing 'It's A Lovely Day Tomorrow', and later introduced a variety of comedy shows, endeavouring to boost our morale.

During my short stay at this camp, I can recall seeing a fellow comrade sweeping up bread crumbs from the ground, after there had been a bread delivery to the camp. On another occasion, I had not been called to work, so I was strolling around the camp with a friend, watching others delousing themselves. We passed the cookhouse and, leaning on the windowsill was the NCO in charge. He yelled at me to go over to him, which we both did. Much to our astonishment, he offered me a loaf of bread in exchange for my cap badge. Much to his disappointment, I refused as I had already promised it to my sister. He was a Sergeant Phillips of the 1st battalion Welsh Guards, and he had been in France long before us.

Each and every day brought a variety of different working parties, and one which I can remember was working in a local nursery garden, where there was an abundance of tomatoes, ripe and unripe; this was, of course, like a king's ransom to us. When the opportunity arose, needless to say, we helped ourselves to the forbidden fruit, and without making it too obvious, we placed some inside our battle dress blouses, with the full intention of bartering them for an extra slice of bread. This was always providing that we managed to get through the camp enclosure entrance, as the Germans would make a search. Through sheer luck and guidance from above, I kept on the working party for a couple of days. Being a small party of just ten to fifteen men, we had an understanding not to arouse any suspicion from the guards. So we did not overload ourselves with spoils, and, fortunately, we got away with it each time.

On returning to camp one evening, and going to my sleeping quarters, I was pleasantly surprised to discover that a newcomer had arrived a few hours earlier and decided to bed down in a bunk below me. Better still, he was a Welsh Guardsman, who had also been captured at Boulogne, but had been on the run, trying to get back home. Eventually, he had been captured and had the good fortune of getting work at the local hospital, treating both British and German soldiers. Luckily, he had escaped the long march through France and Belgium in May and June 1940 and also the nightmare experience of starvation and the cattle truck ordeal. Therefore, instead of bartering forbidden fruit, I was able to share it out with a fellow comrade.

We compared our different experiences since leaving Blighty, and then I enlightened him on the dos and don'ts of a large camp, which he was not accustomed to. This was very much appreciated as he had yet to experience its daily ordeals. A bit later and much to my surprise, from out of his bunk he produced a small suitcase. This contained a variety of underwear and shirts of military issue. He had obviously been allowed to keep this, but it would not be for long, as under present conditions, nothing was safe except what you stood up in. He therefore decided that I, too, was to share in his spoils, and I gained an extra shirt, underwear and a towel. One of the hazards of camp life was that you had to leave little or no possessions on your bed space whilst you were away on a working party, unless someone trustworthy was left to keep an eye on them. Unfortunately, the friendship only lasted a matter of days, when I was called upon to join another working party, of twenty-four men, to be transported elsewhere, destination unknown, the following morning, after roll-call.

It was now early September 1940, and following the usual procedure of being searched, we were leaving Fort 17 and being marched to Thorn railway station, which was right opposite the camp. Eventually, we boarded the train and, much to our surprise, we were herded into the passenger coaches, totally on our own, separated from the Polish civilians. On our arrival at Strasbourg station, we were marched through the town and were given a hearty welcome in what seemed to be a Polish military town. Also, our German guards were not hostile towards our welcome. Having marched about four to five miles into the country, we eventually landed in a village school, which was surrounded by barbed wire. This was obviously meant to be our destination. The journey had not been too strenuous, with so little possessions. Having been ordered inside, as before in the other small camp, fresh straw had been laid on the floor and it was up to each man to choose his bed space quickly. The accommodation also had a ground floor kitchen and a small room, and upstairs there was a classroom. The five German guards, to our surprise, were sharing our living quarters with us, with only a small passageway between us. After we had settled in, we were informed by the Feldwebel (his rank was equivalent to a non-commissioned officer in the British army) and his four guards of various ranks that our purpose there was for felling and loading trees from a nearby forest. We were also given the usual orders to behave ourselves and do as we were told, otherwise we would know the consequences.

The facilities open to us were very encouraging: we had fresh water via a hand pump, electricity, a huge stock of dried logs, and also the use of the kitchen, which was a luxury in itself. Most unusually, we did not have a British NCO amongst us; therefore, we had to take it on ourselves to make our own decisions as to cooking, which turned out to be very successful. We were a mixed bag from different regiments, and it appeared that I was the only Welshman. What we did not know at the time and, considering our circumstances, we had been hand picked individually and could never have anticipated that we would be such a happy, courageous and trustworthy body of men.

After all the preliminary procedures, such as finding bed space, introducing ourselves to each other, strolling around our compound, which in this case was very limited, being such a small playground next to the main road, we were sitting outside in small groups, when the German commandant ventured outside and asked in German, of which we now had a fair knowledge, "Is there anyone present capable of packaging a parcel?" I very cautiously and timidly replied in my best German that I could. Immediately I was taken into the guards living quarters, where I was shown a small quantity of food items on the table. These were to be sent to his wife and family in Germany post haste, for two reasons: firstly, for them to receive the contents fresh and, secondly, so as not to be caught. Obviously, packing was second nature to me, having spent all my working life in the shoe trade. The end result was received with such satisfaction that, not only did he engage me to do many more for him and his four charges, but it landed me the prime job of maintaining their quarters, by looking after them in their general appearance, such as washing their clothes and cleaning their boots. This gave me the grand opportunity of using their limited ration of soapflakes, to do my own washing first and theirs last. I also used their boot polish.

The working party's task was classified as heavy work, and we were allowed extra food rations and, again thanks to our guards, we were also subsidised with extra vegetables from nearby farms, which were still occupied by the Polish people.

As time progressed, our understanding of the German language improved and an exceptionally good understanding grew between the guards and ourselves. I was to learn from the officer in charge that he had served in the Great War and had been to London. He was full of praise for our country and was very keen for his daughter, a school teacher in Germany, to learn our language and to visit our country. This was good for us as he held the British in very high regard. The second in command was also a school teacher and was also of the same opinion as his superior officer. This left the other three guards, who, being middle aged, respected our situation as Prisoners of War.

When we had been at this camp for about ten to fourteen days, the second in command went into town on his daily journey for the mail. This was to contain further orders from the higher command, and luckily, on this occasion, there was also some mail for us and I managed to receive three letters. Unfortunately, not all of us were lucky enough to receive mail from home, but mail obviously boosted our moral.

Owing to the nature of the heavy work being done daily, our guards decided to put us into two shifts, one early morning and the other midday. This was greatly appreciated by the boys, including the two doing the cooking. I appreciated my indoor duties, especially as it was now October 1940 and the weather was deteriorating daily. I was at least warm and dry, although I was personally on call all the time.

One morning, the early party had already left when the weather conditions changed rapidly. Sometime during the morning, an urgent SOS was received by the remainder of the camp; an accident had occurred in the forest. A call went out for all hands to venture forth. Much to our relief, no British soldier was involved. We learned later that they had already completed the work for the morning, which was loading three huge tree trunks onto a horse-drawn wagon. On its journey, the load slipped, trapping the German soldier who was driving underneath, thereby causing panic with the horses. In true British spirit, the working parties immediately gave their first thought to the German soldier pinned underneath such a heavy load, without any regard to their own safety. They eventually released him and, much to their relief, he was still breathing but in a bad way. After getting him out, it was decided that work should finish for the day. Everyone was very sad about the whole thing, and we all thanked God that it was not worse, with many more casualties. Once we arrived back at camp, we learned that, sadly, the soldier had died.

For the next few days, both working parties were confined to camp, although we did not know the reason. One day, around mid morning, much to our surprise, there was an arrival of German staff cars. They stopped outside and we were immediately assembled all together, after an order from our camp commandant. This special invasion of high ranking officers shocked us, but more was to follow. They had come to thank us for the courage and humanity we had shown to one of their men and for ignoring the personal danger to ourselves. They also said it was a pleasure to think that they had such British Tommies in their command and that Churchill would certainly be proud of us.

This act of mercy paid off dividends in a very short space of time, as it was obviously noticed that, although our living conditions were good, the nature of the work meant that the men were continuously wet. Within days, a consignment of brand new battledress (blouse and trousers) arrived for each man. Furthermore, it was arranged that we would be periodically taken by German transport to a military convent hospital for hot baths. Unfortunately, during one of these visits to the hospital, we were lined up for injections. These were in the form of a needle inserted under your right breast, but not being in the position to be able to ask what it was for, or refuse it, we just had to take it.

Over the next few days, our daily tasks continued, even though we had the discomfort of those injections.

The colder weather was now approaching, but we were able to light the heating ovens, using the logs and wood provided. The advantage with this was that they would be able to retain their heat for many hours. It was around this time that my attention was drawn to the plight of one of our lads. He showed me his breasts and testicles, which were swollen out of proportion; therefore, I insisted that we should all examine ourselves for any similar signs. Fortunately for all concerned, there were none. It was decided that I should report this man's condition to the German officers in charge. They were surprised at such a result and decided to take the man straight to the hospital. When the guard returned, it was without the patient, and a sad atmosphere spread around us all, including our German guard. All the inquiries to the hospital for any progress fell on deaf ears and, although this was an upsetting incident, we just had to carry on with our daily duties.

By this time, we were having fortnightly mail from home, which helped to lift our morale, especially with the weather so much colder and daylight limited. Our guards also decided that, with Christmas only five weeks away, they wanted to start preparations for the festive season. This would help both groups, as we were missing home, and it would make the best of a bad situation.

Unfortunately, this was not to be, as orders were received that, owing to the extreme cold winter conditions, we would be unable to carry on where we were, and all the efforts by the officer in charge to keep us together in the vicinity and work elsewhere failed. It was a sad day, when we had to pack up our belongings and to see the emotional feelings shown to us by our guards. They all wished us well individually, and they hoped we would have a safe journey back home to England in the not too distant future. These feelings could not be shown to us when we were back amongst our own countrymen. We made our way back to Thorn and were escorted back to Fort 17, which we had left three months earlier.

Having left this camp in warm sunny weather, we were now back there in extremely bitter, cold, wet and frosty weather. What was worse was to see the people who occupied the camp so bedraggled in their clothing and wooden clogs, and looking such a pitiful sight. This was because they had spent the last three months surviving on bare daily rations.

After being checked and searched again, something we had forgotten about, we were marched off to the furthest right hand side of the camp, to a big black shed, which was obviously going to be our future home. This was captivity of the worst order. After eventually finding sleeping space in a lower bunk, which was approximately two inches above floor level, I found that it was wet and cold. There was no alternative but to make the best of a bad situation and, unfortunately, we were all separated, owing to the lack of sleeping spaces.

We were soon to learn the daily routine of an early morning rise to a cup of so-called coffee, to be collected at the cook house. Midday, there was a ladle of soup, which usually consisted of potatoes, swedes, or anything else which had been delivered in the last few days (if you were lucky). Occasionally, you might find yourself with a strand of horsemeat or similar, which was a luxury. Around 4pm we would each receive a bread ration, which consisted of maybe a fourth or fifth of a kilo of bread, this was about two slices, a very small portion of fat and, occasionally, a substitute of so-called cheese or jam. Also, there would be a role call, outside in all weathers, morning and evening, and on no account were we to leave any of our possessions in our bed space.

Gradually, we got accustomed to the routine. We managed

to meet daily with our old friends from the previous work, and we spent our time together. Our main endeavour was to try to avoid going into the same state mentally and physically as some of our fellow countrymen in the camp. To this end, we wanted to get out on a daily working party, in the hope that, by any means necessary, we could secure something extra to eat. Some days, we were successful and other days were just sheer hard work. We were working in the barracks of the in-training German soldiers, doing all manner of work, and our daily ration of watery soup was sent over from the camp. We were allowed a short break to eat it. Invariably, the German troops would also take their meal break at the same time. They got huge amusement out of this and they enjoyed seeing the British Tommy scrambling for their leftovers, which were put into the small bins, ready for throwing away. Although I was very hungry, along with two or three others, we would not give them the satisfaction or the pleasure to see us doing the same.

Back at the camp, it was pathetic to see fellow countrymen quarrelling, fighting and stealing amongst themselves.

Although I had never been blessed with a singing voice, I joined the camp choir, with the sole purpose of having extra 'buckshees', the prisoners password for something extra, which proved successful on two or three occasions.

On Christmas day 1940, much to our surprise, we were each given a small bottle of lager, with the compliments of the German Reich, and we were invited to join the guards in a sing song around the Christmas tree, which they had erected in the camp. It was a huge success, in both the German and English camps. The favourite part for both groups was the singing of 'Silent Night', which ended our first Christmas in captivity.

We had a theme tune, which was sung every night after roll call; this was 'It's a Lovely Day Tomorrow', which was thanks to Company Sergeant Major (CSM) Hamer of the Rifle Brigade, who endeavoured very hard to keep up the morale of everyone in such atrocious conditions.

1941 brought high hopes that things would change for the better, especially when we received a consignment of Red Cross clothing. This was not sufficient for every man; therefore, every section received so many articles each. To make this as fair as possible, names were put into a hat and drawn out, so that some people were very happy, but lots were disappointed. I was one of the lucky ones; I drew a pair of British Army long johns, which were most acceptable for night and day wear, especially as we were only two weeks into the New Year and the middle of winter.

I had managed to get onto a party working on the local aerodrome, where the German pilots were being trained. To get there, we had to march two to three miles outside of Thorn and go over the River Vistula by crossing a huge bridge. We went before dawn every day, and we were able to see the German tanks and heavy armour training on the frozen river, which showed the extent of the bitterly cold weather conditions. On our arrival at the aerodrome, the party of twenty to thirty men would be detailed to brush and keep the runway clear of snow, to enable the planes to land and to take off.

Owing to the security, we were guarded not only by our

own guards but by the air force police as well. All were heavily armed, which meant that once we were given our positions and allocated so many yards to keep free of snow, we were not allowed to leave under any circumstances, or we would be shot. Even to go to the toilet was impossible, so you had to urinate where you stood. Unfortunately, it was so cold that, before the urine hit the ground, it had frozen, but luckily, I had my Red Cross underpants, which were a Godsend as my battle dress was getting threadbare by now.

I also still had my great coat (the one I had previously swapped), which, although short, was still a great help at keeping me warm. We had a midday break, when we were allowed to sit in a hanger, but we had no food. The young German airmen were delighted to be able to laugh and giggle at us as they threw odd pieces of bread in amongst us and watched our boys fighting and scrambling for the food. Along with a few others, I refused to satisfy their delight, just stood my ground and ignored their antics, although sometimes the hunger pains were very hard to resist.

On our return each evening at dusk, we were lined up for our bowl of watery soup and our bread ration, which the rest had had at midday. We then returned indoors, which was crowded with fellow prisoners huddled together for warmth, but to us it was warm compared to the blizzard we had faced all day.

Every night, I returned to my bottom bunk, which was a few wooden boards only inches from the sodden ground, knowing that in a few minutes I would be fast asleep under my blanket and my great coat, having removed my boots and kept them by my side. However tired or hungry I was each night, I still thanked God in a silent prayer for surviving another day. After thankfully surviving seven days, our party was completely changed and given other duties. I was fortunate and was able to avoid all working parties for the next seven to ten days, and remained in camp.

One day, lying in my bed, my rest was disturbed by a trickle of water coming from the bunk above. I automatically rolled out to investigate the cause. Much to my astonishment and dismay, when I shook the occupier, to wake him up, he had passed away. Along with some of the others, we removed his body and belongings to the medical hut. On my return, I immediately promoted myself to his bunk, as it was higher off the ground. This had its down side: it was within easier reach for the German guards to give a waking dig with whatever they had in their hands at the time, usually a rifle butt. At least the new bunk was much drier than the one below.

Some of our fellow countrymen had the very good fortune to be sleeping in the fort barracks where the Polish soldiers resided. The living conditions were much warmer and drier there. We were very envious and it was our soul ambition to get in if it was at all possible. I was not able to get there, and had to be content in the big black hut.

As at this time I was not in a working party and able to have a rest, I was able to catch up on some of my own odd jobs, one being washing out my long johns in cold water. I hung them out to dry on the chimney breast, although I kept an eagle eye on them at all times. I left them there once, and whilst I turned my back for a second, much to my cost, on my return, they had disappeared, therefore, I was without my extra warmth. During the next few days, I had a variety of jobs, along with others, in and around the town of the Thorn, in different barracks.

The main attraction now was that, all day and all through the night, we had train loads of German soldiers and materials passing through, heading for the eastern front, in Russia. What amazed us most was the amount of war material that had been allowed to be stored in preparation for the war. When we were in England, we had nothing.

Although the work was varied and in many cases heavy, it was a means of getting out of the camp. This took us away from the atmosphere of defeat and of seeing our fellow countrymen in such deplorable state of mind. The favourite song in camp at this time was 'Underneath the Arches', sung by Flannigan and Allen, but our version was 'Underneath the Arches We Delouse our Time Away'.

German planes regularly flying high above, trousers for my pillow, and body lice being a great menace to us all (the last having been brought about by the atrocious living conditions), I was very relieved when, towards the end of January 1941, my name and number were called out by the camp messenger, and I was told to report to the office immediately, with my full possessions. These only consisted of a dixie can, spoon, blanket (which was threadbare), a small piece of towel and, last but not least, a shaving brush and two packets of razor blades. The latter were purchased with my camp money, on the few occasions when the canteen was open with supplies. As requested, I reported to the office and was told I would be leaving at the crack of dawn, for a working party, destination unknown, and that I was to stay in a nearby hut, ready to be collected by the guard in the morning. Once again, I did not know what the future held, but I was grateful to be getting away from such conditions, whatever was in store.

Before the crack of dawn, I was marched away to join the four other colleagues who were going, too. One of these, much to my surprise, was a senior NCO, who was in charge of Stalag XXA Fort 17; his name was CSM Hamer of the London Rifle Brigade. The three others were a corporal and a private from the RAMC, and an interpreter by the name of Cliff, from another regiment. We were marched off with an armed guard to Thorn railway station, opposite the camp.

After travelling all day, with numerous changes, we eventually arrived after dark at Grupper station. We were then marched (much to our delight) only a matter of minutes down the road, where we entered a huge military garrison. We passed through to the furthest point, where there was barbed wire, a very familiar scene. It was fairly obvious that we were in a fairly large camp, and although everywhere was under snow and everything frozen, our living quarters were Nissen huts. Being the odd one out in the party, due to rank, and still only a so-called cobbler, I was taken to a room with about twenty men inside. The four others, being of higher ranks, were taken elsewhere.

The lighting in the hut was dim; there was only a single oil lamp, but despite this, I was soon surrounded by my fellow countrymen and was questioned continually about how the war was going and the latest happenings from my previous camp. Filling in to the best of my ability details of my old camp, which was not very encouraging, and telling them about the food and living conditions, I found that this camp was not very much better, and that it was close to mutiny, as no one seemed to be in control. Therefore, they were pleased to get the news that CSM Hamer had arrived with us, as he was well known for controlling Fort 17, which consisted of more than one thousand men, and at this camp there were around one hundred. Also, the work consisted of working in and around the German occupied garrison, which had previously been held by the Polish military. It appeared that, owing to a lack of supply of Red Cross parcels and letters, food rations were not equally divided, which was causing a near mutiny, and the consequences of this were that people could be shot. I then realised why CSM Hamer had been sent with us, but I was puzzled as to why I had been sent; when I said I was a camp cobbler, I was informed that they already had one.

One good thing about being sent here was that the barrack room was equipped with discarded Polish, two-tier iron beds, which was a blessing in disguise. After giving them all my information, I prepared for the luxury of sleeping in a single bed, which was so different to sleeping on the wooden planks in the previous place.

Long before daybreak, we had the normal early morning call, which was the same everywhere, although here we did not have the long queues for the so-called morning coffee, which still bore no resemblance to the real thing. If you were lucky, you had a slice or two of bread, which you had managed to save from the previous night's rations.

Following the departure of the whole camp to various places of work, there was just a handful of people left behind, who were the camp staff. These consisted of the CSM, twin medical orderlies, two or three cooks, a tailor, one man to look after the German guards, and me, the cobbler. The job of looking after the guards was a position envied by all. I knew because I had previously done this myself, before going on working parties.

We were taken to our new workroom, where the tools of our trade were laid out, which were the same as before and consisted of one hammer, pincers, a knife, wooden pegs, split legs, hob nails and small pieces of leather. With all this I was expected to keep my fellow comrades' boots in good repair, especially for a full inspection of clothing and boots on a Sunday morning. The new tailor and I were very embarrassed when we found out we had displaced the previous person, who was called Bob Jackson, No 6060, from Warwickshire, who was a far better tradesman than either of us. He was a professional, but on no account would he take our place, as we had been sent specially by the German high command in Thorn to do the jobs.

Following our usual procedure of teaming off with a fellow 'muckerin' (partner) to share fifty-fifty of whatever came your way, I thought I was quite lucky to be chummed up with a fellow Welshman from North Wales, who was serving in the 1st Battalion of the Welsh Guards. Thanks to the influence of CSM Hamer, a change was brought about on military discipline, including the German guards, who, it appeared, had been very trigger happy before. Much to the relief of everyone, in a matter of fourteen days, he had managed to arrange a delivery of Red Cross parcels and cigarettes; this consisted of one parcel between every two or three men, which made the conditions a little easier, if only temporarily. Feelings were now running high, with all the extra food, cigarettes and everything. Everybody was happier, with the exception of myself, when it was brought to my notice that my fellow countryman was helping himself to the 'Kim' dried milk when my back was turned, and that was an unforgivable crime in these circumstances, so I discontinued my friendship with him. This worked in my favour, as, in the not too distant future, a replacement arrived from the main camp in Thorn, in the form of another Welshman, called Raymond Rich, who came from Watton garage in Brecon, and who was in the Queen's Regiment. By good fortune, I was able to barter for a top bunk next to mine for him, but this friendship was unavoidably to end after many months of sharing everything by half, through good times and bad, when Raymond was urgently taken away, and later repatriated due to ill health.

This was a severe blow to me, as by now I had changed my job from being a cobbler, which I hated, to working in the camp guards' barracks. I repaired and polished their jack boots to such a high standard that I was given the opportunity to take over from a Scotsman, who, for some unknown reason, was called back to Thorn. This was beneficial, as I was able to keep my own underwear and things clean and fresh by using the German guards' issue of soap flakes before washing theirs.

During the year 1941, we heard of the loss of the British ships, one of which was the *Prince of Wales,* and the bombing of Singapore. This boosted the Germans morale and lowered ours.

By this time, a fair trickle of regular mail was being received, with a variety of news, such as the wives and girlfriends 'finding' babies on their doorsteps and having to take them in, in the hope that their partners would accept them after the war; sympathetic stories, lots of messages to finish courtships as the women had found someone else. Some of these were very long friendships indeed, and others were rekindled. We were perplexed because we were unaware of the number of American GIs that had been stationed in our country.

Although living conditions were better, food was still in short supply and when eventually a Red Cross parcel did arrive, an order was issued by the German high command that all parcels were to be stored under lock and key in the guards' accommodation. After work each evening, small parties were marched off to collect their requirements, but before returning to camp, each and every tin was punctured open and its contents emptied into whatever dish or dixie one had with them, which meant you had a stew with jam or jelly all mixed up. The reason for this was so that no prisoner could store away any extra food for escaping. Fortunately, this procedure was brought to the attention of the Red Cross and the guards were told to stop.

Early in the winter of 1941, we were moved to the very centre of the German compound, into a disused barracks, which was a luxury as it had electric light and a modern cookhouse. This had previously been used by Polish and German troops, so the beds were still two-tier and, owing to my position and the fact that I was on call at all times, I was allocated a small room attached to the cookhouse. This room had four beds, and I shared it with the camp tailor and interpreter. This was a complete luxury compared to the other huts. There was a second room like this on the other side of the cookhouse, and this is where CSM Hamer slept, along with the medical orderlies and the four cooks, as by now our camp numbers had increased.

One of the duties of the German guard who patrolled the camp at night, was to wake the cooks and for them to then make sure that I was awake by 6.30 am. I was expected to be on duty in the German guard room, to attend the German Commandant and his secretary. This was to do things like bed-making. When I had completed the tasks for the Commandant, I was expected then to do likewise in two other rooms, where the guards slept. During this time, I was allowed a treat, which was to listen to Lord Haw Haw doing his daily propaganda announcements, and I was encouraged to go back to barracks to tell our boys what he had said.

Daily routine was much of a muchness, day in and day out. Daily rations were still very limited, more so because there were no outside jobs for the boys and so there was no opportunity to acquire extra rations.

It was during the early part of November 1941 that we had a few extra fellow countrymen join us, one of whom (luckily for us) was a very experienced 1914-1918 war veteran and ex Prisoner of War, who was put in charge of us and our German guards. It was at this time that three of our boys foolishly tried to escape, but they were quickly recaptured, in just a matter of hours, by our own German guards, in the woods that bordered our camp. The higher German command and the Gestapo were aware of the matter and, as a punishment, the following Sunday, which was the nearest to our Armistice Day, 11th November, the German commandant had no alternative but to put the whole camp on a punishment parade. This meant that our only rest day was taken up with digging and general duties around the camp. This punishment continued for some weeks. However, within the first three hours on that first Sunday, there was a nasty incident involving an ex Welsh guardsman by the name of Thomas, who was from Neath, South Wales, and who stood over six feet tall. Thomas had come in with the last group of prisoners and I had befriended him. He was also the ex battalion boxing champion. Thomas was working with a group digging a trench some ten yards from the guards' quarters. Unfortunately, this group had the worst possible guard in charge of them. This guard had been injured in the head whilst fighting in Russia and was known to be trigger-happy. During the course of the morning, I was carrying out my duties at the commandant's office, overlooking the lads working. I overheard and saw an argument brewing between guardsman Thomas and trigger happy Jo. I had only just got to the doorway when I heard a rifle shot and I saw Thomas go down. Immediately, I ran over and, to my shock and horror, as he raised his head and shoulders I noticed that, underneath his balaclava, the whole of the lower half of his jaw had been blown away. My immediate response, while kneeling and supporting him, was to turn to the guard and call him a German bastard. His response was to ask me if I wanted the same. By the grace of God, the commandant shouted from his quarters at this point, and saved the situation.

Although Guardsman Thomas was taken away by the German medical orderlies, as soon as they could, we were later told that he had passed away. Though, as quite often happened, a few months later, news came to us that this was untrue and he had been repatriated.

This incident caused a heavy atmosphere over the whole camp, including the German guards. It also gave an example of how futile and foolish it was to attempt any escape, and we were very lucky that our circumstances were not worse, especially if the German high command had known anything about it. The other thing to come out of this incident was that the German guard was mysteriously spirited away and never returned. His replacement was a German Wesleyan minister, who had been brought into the German army much against his beliefs, and he got very attached to me, especially when he understood that I was also a Wesleyan.

Strictly against German regulations, this ex-minister secretly passed to me his rifle for cleaning, as he was a man of religion and he was too scared of handling the weapon himself. He was very appreciative and showed this by rewarding me with bread and extra food from his daily ration.

Christmas 1941 had now come and gone and, thankfully, the Red Cross parcels had arrived and been shared, with one parcel between four people.

Spring 1942 brought the news that we were going to be returned to our original small camp on the outskirts of a forest, and thereby splitting the camp in half. When the move was completed, we were down to around forty men, which made things easier all round. Our British Company Sergeant Major Hamer was returned to Thorn, and his replacement was the CSM of a Scottish regiment, who proved to be very successful.

It was at this time, whilst carrying out my duties in the German quarters, that I heard the sad news on the German radio that Singapore had fallen. This was reinforced the following morning by Lord Haw Haw's broadcast, which was played for my benefit, so that I could take the news back to camp, although my fellow comrades had been told and invited to listen to it with the German troops in their quarters. This boosted the morale of our enemy, especially alongside their success in Russia.

We were not surprised at these successes; our lads were witnessing daily what the Germans were able to transport into Russia, both men and machines. During the next few months, their morale was riding high; we were certainly the underdogs and under the impression that England would be their next target and achievement.

During the early summer of 1942, the Red Cross parcels had become fewer, and by the order of the German High Command, we were not allowed to just take the parcels into our camp, to use as we wished, they were to be left in the German quarters and collected when required, after work in the evening. Each tin was then opened by the German guards, before they were handed over to us. This was done because some British boys were accumulating food and chocolate for escape purposes. This order was carried out through all

British POW camps, and it meant we were only given limited amounts and had to share them between six people instead of four. Fortunately, this arrangement did not last for very long as it meant the guards had to supervise the opening of the tins, and the quality of these rations was superior to their own.

Daily, I would take back to the camp a report of what I had heard broadcast from Lord Haw Haw. Sometimes, he would name individuals who had been captured in Crete and the desert, and he would also talk about the great advancement they were making against British troops.

As the summer progressed, one day we were informed that a train load of Russian Prisoners of War would be staying at the sidings nearby. We were told that we could help them as much as we wanted to during the short time that they were there. We arranged to forfeit some of our own potato and cabbage rations, which were made into a soup. It was not much but it boosted the German ration as well. The whole camp volunteered to help, as, having spent days ourselves in cattle trucks, we knew full well what the conditions were like. Unfortunately, only a small party were allowed out to assist. Maybe this was all for the best, as on their return, they told us about the conditions and the state these fellow human beings were in. We ourselves had experienced bad times, but nothing in comparison to what our boys and the German guards had seen that day. Apparently, human bones were lying around, meaning that human flesh had been eaten. Regrettably, we felt we should have given them more, although we did not have enough food ourselves. That experience remained with us for a very long time, and we thought about it each and every day.

In mid September, I was to accompany my German minister, when he went to collect our letters from the local post office. Having been handed the bundle and while waiting for the return of the guard, I started looking for my own mail. I found one letter addressed to me, and was naturally anxious to read the contents, written by my sister from Aberdare. I started reading. I only had a few minutes to scan the letter, only to read that my mother had passed away on August 4th, 1942, two days after her birthday, and had been laid to rest in Machynlleth, North Wales, her home surroundings. This was a great shock as I did not know that my mother had been ill. She had been suffering for months, from around the time I was listed as missing in 1940. My guard recognised that something was wrong, due to the expression on my face, which explained all. When I returned to camp, I can only remember lying on my bed and remaining there for the next few hours, until duty called for me to do my evening routine at the commandant's and guards' rooms.

It was during this time that a certain special German skiing battalion were stationed in the nearby garrison and were daily passing our camp. We noticed that they wore a white flower in their caps, which we found out was edelweiss, and years later, whenever I heard the popular song played back in Britain, it brought back lots of memories.

During the next few weeks, work seemed to carry on as usual, until early November, when we were moved back into the centre of the garrison, to occupy the hut we had previously occupied. Fortunately, we had the same commandant and guards as before, which made things much easier for us all. Our new CSM of the Scottish Black Watch was a keen disciplinarian and liked law and order. This was to prove essential in the not to distant future, as it got back to him that there was a homosexual amongst us. He solved this problem, and all was back to normal, with everyone carrying on in the usual manner, although our rations had been cut again.

By now, my duties had increased a little, by looking after the German Officer and his secretary, and I was to be allowed an extra pair of hands, so I put this to our own camp commander, and he chose another Scottish man, one with bright red hair, whose nickname was Ginger. I found him quite an asset, although he was a bit short tempered at times and I had to control him.

The German Commandant and his secretary were always appreciative of how the camp was being run, and more so of Ginger and me, on how we kept everything running smoothly in the German quarters. The Commandant had himself been a Prisoner of War in the 1914-1918 war, and had been treated well, so he tried to do likewise, as far as possible, for us.

It was around this time that a German officer developed a close friendship with a Polish woman, and had somehow managed to get her living in a single hut, which was alongside the guards' quarters and ours. Eventually, I was brought into the picture and it was arranged that I would, on certain days, when told, take over a canister of hot water in the morning and again mid afternoon. This journey was a few hundred yards and had to be done alone. I also had a picnic in disguise. After the first two or three journeys, I was invited in, and the woman smothered me in hugs and kisses and called me Great Engländer. Her knowledge of German was very poor and, if anything, mine was better.

As time progressed, going back, I found that my empty canister always contained something extra, like egg sandwiches, bits of sausages and a slice or two of white bread. This had to be kept confidential as I knew that the extra was coming from the German officer. I was certainly onto a good thing. Needless to say, I looked forward to my errands of mercy, and it appeared that she was a Polish refugee, in a similar predicament to myself and doing what she needed to do in order to stay alive.

During the harsh months of November, December and the first three months of the New Year (1943), priority was given to snow clearing, and our days were limited as the darkness fell early. Camp life was just work and sleep, and we were quite unaware of what was happening in the outside world and the progress of the war. We did manage to get a trickle of information, which was telling us that things were improving for us, and there were signs of a tremendous amount of heavy troop movements around the garrison.

With the arrival of Christmas 1942, and the severe weather conditions, the signs were that things were not going as well for the Germans as Lord Haw Haw claimed. He was still doing his daily broadcasts, telling us all the German achievements, but we had it on good authority that we were by now having more success with our bombing raids on Berlin and other cities, and that our land forces were also having some success. The tide was turning in our favour, which was proved by the amount of troops and equipment passing through our garrison, and where we worked, and all our rules and regulations were being tightened.

Early spring again meant that we were to be divided back into our original small party and go back to our small camp. The remainder of our fellow men were to return to Thorn, which meant that our guards were also reduced in numbers. This left me to carry on, on my own, single-handedly in the German quarters.

Red Cross parcels were very slow in arriving, practically non existent, but the service of our mail and individual parcels seemed to be improving. I, at this time, seemed to have a fair amount of letters sympathising with me over the loss of my mother in August 1942. Bad news came again in these letters, telling me that my cousin Henry Evans had been lost at sea, which naturally hurt me, as he was younger than I by two to three years. At least, to date, I had survived.

One late spring evening, when a working party returned, there was rather a lot of activity to greet them; a message had been received via our camp commandant that a quantity of films were missing from the German headquarters, and knowing full well that Engländers were employed around the garrison, he thought that the most likely culprit was one of them. Before being admitted into the camp, they were stopped and lined up, as was the usual procedure, but this time they were held for longer, and our CSM was brought to the German headquarters, to explain what had happened. Fortunately for all concerned, we had the same commandant and guards, which worked very much in our favour. It was explained that what had happened was a serious offence, and that every man had to be searched for these negatives, unless they were voluntarily handed over. The CSM addressed the men outside, to appeal for the culprit or culprits to hand the films over, to save any further serious punishment, as they would not be allowed into camp. He was not ordering, but appealing for common sense to prevail, for everyone's sake. Consequently, the negatives were handed over to him, to give back to the German Officer, much to the relief of all concerned. The working party were then allowed back into the camp.

What was unknown to anybody, apart from me, was that, during my evening tour of duty, while tidying up the commandant's clerk's desk, I spotted the offending negatives, and I accidentally flicked a few near to me on the floor. I quickly scooped them up into my pocket, offering up a silent prayer that there were too many to be missed from the few I had taken. When the first opportunity occurred for me to look at what I had taken, I noticed that I had five negatives and, to my horror, I noticed that Hitler was on one. I now realized that I was holding vital evidence, and that it would take some explaining if they were ever found in my possession. Thankfully, this never happened as it would certainly have meant the firing squad. There remained two options for me: either to destroy or keep the negatives. I chose the latter and decided to hide the negatives in a razor blade packet, due to their small size. Although I was in the habit of sharing food with my fellow comrades, I decided not to get anyone else involved, so that, if they should be found, I would be the only one in trouble.

The mail from home was now becoming more regular,

including clothing parcels, but the main thing we were looking for was news of the war. So we all asked each other if they had news, and although this was normally blanked out with censor's ink, I managed to get a word or two in Welsh from my sister that the censor missed because he could not understand it. We were still getting some Red Cross parcels, although not many, but the orders from German high command had been relaxed slightly, so that all the tins were opened at once and distributed, whereas at one time, they were being wasted. There were fewer parcels than before, but they still had to be shared between all of the POWs. Our normal rations were still only one loaf between four or five men, but we were still better off than our fellow men in the larger camps. Our working conditions and sleeping quarters were luxury compared to many others. Nevertheless, I still thanked God every night for surviving another day.

At this time, a Welshman arrived at our camp, and what was most unusual was that he was a seaman. He was from the Merchant Navy and I believe he was picked up around 1941/1942. He gave us more up to date information on how things were progressing. I befriended him, as he was a Welshman from Penrhyndeudraeth in North Wales and was inclined to be a very quiet, shy and reserved person. I had been fortunate that at this time I had a clothing parcel from home and I was able to share some with him, as up to this date he had not received any mail. We nicknamed him Sailor (this seemed the most obvious) and he was soon in our little group, sharing any extra food that we had obtained through fair means or foul from the Germans. He appreciated everything we did.

As time went by, his sister-in-law, who was attached to the St John Ambulance, wrote to me regularly. Her letters were very humorous and full of jokes, so we looked forward to receiving them, but they embarrassed Sailor very much as he was so shy.

Towards late spring, rumours began to spread that we were to return to the larger camp at Thorn. This proved to be correct and we returned towards the end of May 1943. It had been two and a half years since we had left fort 17, in Thorn, Poland.

The weather conditions had improved; summer was coming, with warm and bright sunny days, a definite contrast to January 1942, when the temperature was well below freezing, with snowdrifts and everything frozen.

On arrival at the camp, the normal procedures were enforced and all our belongings were searched. Naturally, I was shaking in my boots and keeping my fingers crossed that the negatives in my possession would not be found. By the grace of God, we were allowed through into the special wired compound and then into the main camp, without my secret being discovered. Luckily, we were sent to the opposite end of the camp to when we were there before, which was in early 1941, and we had stayed in a horrible huge black shed, where we lived like animals in rat-infested, wet, cold and miserable conditions. This time, we were sent to new surroundings in the shape of a hut which had three-tier individual bunks, which was a great improvement. It also meant that we had more space, unlike last time, when lack of space made us argue and be very short tempered.

Syd as a young recruit with the 2nd Battalion
Welsh Guards on 17th February 1940.

Syd (on left) in Stalag XXA Thorn Poland. Card created 25th November 1941, but it looks like summer.

Syd (bottom row on right), on initial training in 1940 at Caterham Barracks, the headquarters of the Guards training from 1850–1990.

Syd (bottom row, 3rd from left) in Stalag XXA Thorn, Poland. Concentration camps were designed to exploit the prisoners for labout. Many died from disease, starvation, exhaustion or were executed.

Prisoner of War camp, probably at Thorn, Poland.

Syd (2nd row, 3rd from right) and fellow Welsh Guards recruits in 1940. The 2nd Battalion were formed on 18th May 1939 and were a hostilities only unit. This Battalion was placed in suspended animation after the end of the war.

Syd in training at Roman Way Camp, Colchester before being deployed to France in 1940 as part of the British Expeditionary Force.

Syd paying his respects in 1999 at St Martin's church, Boulogne. The war graves include twelve Welsh guardsmen killed in action in 1940.

Syd (fourth from left) at Stalag XXA, Thorn, Poland. At its peak this complex contained 20,000 men.

A card showing Syd as a Prisoner of War at
Stalag XXA, sent to his uncle and aunt in
Penegoes, Machynlleth on September 16th,

Syd (kneeling) at Stalag XXA, Thorn. This camp
began in late 1939.

A stolen negative from the commandant clerk's office.

Another stolen negative showing a German military vehicle.

A stolen negative of Wehrmacht gunners. Close to 16 million served in the Wehrmacht between 1939 and 1945.

A stolen negatice of marching "gerry". The Allies
dissolved the German army in August 1946.

A stolen negative of Hitler and his designated
successor Hermann Goering, one of the creators of
the concentration camps.

Syd in Welsh Guards ceremonial tunic. The
Welsh Guards tunic is distinguished by its
buttons in groups of five.

Syd with his "Aunty Dats" (Catherine Jane Powles)
from Penegoes, Machynlleth at his home, Brynmair
Rd., Godreaman, Aberdare.

Syd (standing) and a fellow prisoner at Stalag XXA Thorn,
Poland. Thorn was a sub camp to the Sztutowic camp.

Syd (on the right) and another Prisoner of War, probably at Stalag XXA, Thorn. Thorn was liberated from the Nazis by the Soviet Red Army in 1945.

Syd (on the right) and fellow detainees, possibly in Thorn camp.

Syd at his home in Brynmair Rd., Godreaman, Aberdare.

Syd in ceremonial tunic and wearing his cap and
badge. The Welsh Guards came into existence
in February 1915, the last of the foot guard
divisions to be created. Their motto is "Cymru
am Byth".

Syd in uniform. He served from 29th December 1939 until
January 1946 with the 2nd Battalion Welsh Guards.

There was a new daily routine to get used to, which started right away. Our daily issue of bread did not change, still being between five men, but we had to start new sharing arrangements, with complete strangers. The daily roll call meant we all had to line up in fives to be counted. From long experience, I knew that this could take a couple of hours, especially if the numbers did not tally with the German guards' register. One bright spot during roll call was that any letters from home were called out, so that we got our news then.

The days and weeks that were to follow were totally different and difficult after our recent spell of "luxury", when we had been accustomed to the free and easy style of food distribution at our last camp and also knowing everyone by name. Instead, we had to start queuing again for the so-called coffee that was served in the morning and for a ladle full of so-called soup (this was very watery) at midday.

The daily routine here was one of small working parties being taken out from the camp and sent to work in various parts of the town of Thorn. However, since my last stay at this camp in 1941, when we wore all manner of uniforms, and wooden clogs on our feet, there was one big improvement in the appearance of my fellow countrymen (with the exception of a certain few). A new issue had come through from the Red Cross of British uniforms, including boots, which made us more look respectable and more like British soldiers. When combined with parcels from home, we were the envy of the German guards, especially as they were looking the worse for wear with their uniforms.

Other things that were happening at this time were that the

German guards were busy buying coffee, tea and chocolates on the black market, at very good prices, to send home to their families in Germany, and we were lucky enough to start getting entertainment. This was very popular and we started to get weekly shows, with musical instruments supplied by the Red Cross. This entertainment was really good and it was surprising the incredible range of talented artists who were amongst the lads in the camp; even the German guards attended the shows regularly. The signature tune of the show was 'It's a Lovely Day Tomorrow', and we also sang the national anthem, 'God Save the King'. On Sundays there was a church service and this was fully attended. We had hymn books and bibles, supplied by the Red Cross.

Our hut was situated just on the other side of Thorn's main railway station and it was fascinating to see and hear, both night and day, all the movement of troops and equipment on these trains, and the general talk was about the second front and when and where it would take place.

Each and everyday meant something different. If by chance you remained in camp, it was encouraging to see how the majority of men either casually walked around the camp, or went into the barracks where dominoes, Ludo, bridge and whist were being played. Sometimes these card games were played in complete silence and with an air of seriousness, especially when some were played for a huge amount of camp money on the turn of just one card. These games would command a large audience, with great excitement on the outcome.

The majority of the men had been on all manner of working parties, many miles from Thorn, and because of this, their appearance and condition was such that they coped really well with our present surroundings.

June and July brought very warm weather, and each day brought in a variety of jobs, some within the camp and, on other days, jobs outside. It was also now possible to leave your belongings on your bed space and they would be untouched and quite safe until your return.

One day, I got on a working party that was working in Thorn, at a nursery garden, which was really good as it was an opportunity to help ourselves to all manner of food that was available there. The easiest things to take were tomatoes and, within reason, we took some back to camp, to exchange for extra bread, margarine, jam or whatever else was available.

On my return one day, I found that what had been an empty bed next to me had been taken by a complete stranger. So, I went into the usual procedure of asking the basic questions: his name, regiment, where captured etc. Much to my astonishment, I learnt that he was a Welsh guardsman, captured in Boulogne two days before me. Apparently, he had remained in Boulogne until just a few weeks before being transferred here. He had been working all those years in a local hospital, nursing German soldiers. Our other lads, it appeared, along with all the other regiments, had been transferred, or buried early in 1940.

I was astonished at the amount of clothing and knickknacks he had in his possession, along with a very expensive suitcase. He explained that he had been extremely lucky; because he had been a long term prisoner, he had been allowed to live in semi-luxury and had avoided the weeks of marching through

France to the Belgian border and the confinement in the cattle trucks with forty or fifty others. Although we were in the same battalion, we had never met or seen each other before. When comparing our stories, I found out that he had been captured on the Thursday, whilst Jeff and I managed to last out until the Saturday.

After we had discussed our histories, I briefed him on the daily camp routine, what to do, what to avoid, and it became obvious that he was not accustomed to this more confined way of surviving. Our friendship didn't last long as he was drafted to another working party and sent elsewhere. This was a pity really, as he spoke fluent German, but before he left, he insisted on giving me a huge French nightshirt, which later came in very handy, and some smaller items. I was deeply sorry to see him go, as I'm sure we would have become great friends and been able to confide in each other.

I was still receiving a fair amount of mail from home, either from relatives or friends, like my girlfriend from my Sunday school days, Bronwen, which was a pleasant surprise, as our friendship had lasted on and off for years, although it was not serious.

Each and every day brought something different, but on one occasion, I was lucky to get on a guardroom working party, where there was an abundance of home grown tomatoes, although I had never eaten tomatoes before the war, I certainly made up for all those years now and, furthermore, being discreet, I carried a good supply back into camp, where I was able to barter them for extra bread or anything else useful. This carried on for five days or more, until one day, when my number was called out with others to report to the office; we were leaving camp to work on the estate farm the next day.

Next morning, I found myself with twenty-three other fellow countrymen going on the same party. Three or four of the boys I recognised from previous working parties.

At this time, I had mixed feelings about leaving this camp, mostly because things were so well organised in everything, such as the distribution of rations and Red Cross parcels when they arrived, also the religious services, entertainment and sport. This was so very different to my last stay here in 1940/1941, when everything was the survival of the fittest. Also, apart from a few undesirable individuals who let the British Tommies down, the majority of us, having been issued with new uniforms, great coats and boots, which along with the clothing parcels from home, were putting the Germans soldiers to shame. By now, they were beginning to look very shabby. Their attitude towards us had also improved, apart from the odd soldier, which I put down to the war news being daily in our favour.

Before our departure to the station, in September 1943, the German procedure was still the same: we were lined up and checked and obviously searched. It was at this point that I always crossed my fingers and held my breath until they passed onto the next person, which was when I gave a huge sigh of relief that the ordeal was over again. As usual, we were given a loaf of bread, to be shared between five or six (whatever the order for the day was), which would mean two or three slices each. By now we were quite civilised and would wait for our portion and not demand it from whoever was distributing it. In the past, due to our extreme hunger, we would not trust each other and would scramble, push and fight amongst ourselves until we received our share. At this point, our four new German guards marched us through the two heavy steel doors on our way to Thorn railway station. My thoughts and daydreams had often pictured the Russian troops barging in through those doors and liberating us. Now, we were on our way to an unknown destination.

Fortunately, the railway station was opposite the camp, although it meant a detour of about fifteen minutes to get onto the platforms, which was annoying as we were carrying a fair amount of clothing and other things in boxes, suitcases and haversacks. The civilian population were kept away from us (they used to drop titbits for us), but that did not stop us from dropping the occasional cigarette or piece of soap for them, nothing too obvious, in case our guards saw. With all the entrances cleared for us, we were able to pass the keen eyes of the SS and railway police and walk onto the central platform. Most unusually for the Prisoners of War, the railway arrangements were second to none, with the postal arrangements for delivering our mail from home already in place, as moving camp always caused problems. On this occasion, there seemed to be a different set up, as the trains going to our destination did not have the cattle trucks that we always travelled in attached at the rear. We did not move until early afternoon and, this time, we were overjoyed to see that we were to be loaded into normal civilian coaches. Needless to say, our guard was strengthened.

Having travelled for some hours, we were obliged to

change trains at a busy junction. After some time of waiting, we were again put into civilian carriages, after they had been cleared of civilians, which was a luxury to us. Someone had, in the meantime, found out that we were going to a state farm. This did not bother me as I was fortunate to have spent summer holidays in the countryside and was accustomed to the animals and daily routine, whereas many of the lads had no idea of farm work.

By the time we arrived at our small railway station destination, darkness had fallen and we were marched approximately two miles along a cobbled road, eventually arriving in a little village called, I believe, Gut' Delau. We were then directed to a building which was above a cow shed, but, much to our astonishment, it was spotlessly clean, with whitewashed walls, bunk beds, a huge stove, tables, chairs and electric light, a great luxury. We even had wooden wash basins fixed to the walls and a kitchen converted for use. Although there were twenty-four of us sharing this room, it was still far more comfortable than the last big camp.

After each man had chosen his bunk bed, the next thing was to brew up a cup of tea in the kitchen, and, having been told by our three remaining guards, that we would be called early in the morning for our farm duties, we went to bed.

The following morning, we all gathered in the farmyard and it appeared that we were the first British Prisoners of War to have been seen by the Polish villagers. Like us, they were gathered on one side of the farmyard (we were on the opposite side), waiting to be detailed off to various jobs on the farm. It was obvious to us that the Germans had given them a list of rules and regulations and warned them that on no account were they to talk to us or get near to us, and if they were caught the consequences would be severe punishment, and we knew only too well what this amounted to. It would appear that this would be the daily routine for allocation of work, as some of our lads, who had previously worked on state farms, told us.

It now came to our turn to be detailed about our jobs by the two Polish foremen. We were each given different farm tools, which were a surprise to many of the men as they were very old fashioned working tools. As I had played around on farms as a child in North Wales, many of the tools were familiar to me and I knew their uses. With only two German guards, we were divided into two working parties and then marched out into the fields, leaving behind two men in the camp as cooks.

During the course of the day, from various tasks, we were able to gather from our guard that our sole purpose would be to gather in the harvest in due course, which meant potato picking, sugar beet gathering and harvesting other vegetables, to be transported into Germany. This recent information proved to be correct as the following weeks confirmed, and also by the German guards, who were of the older generation and more sympathetic to us all.

We settled in quickly and became firm favourites of the village folk (there were always ways and means), and by mysterious ways, of the baron and his family who were true Germans, and had now, for the German Reich, taken over the farm from the previous Polish owner, as was the case in all of Poland and elsewhere.

The family consisted of the baron, his wife, the baroness, a daughter and a son, who were about our ages. Living there also was the baron's mistress and her family, who were Ukrainians. This family consisted of a mother and father of the older generation, the son and daughter, the latter, being the senior, was in her late twenties and the friend of the baron.

The old gent (baron) was kept fully occupied on the farm, whilst his son (amongst other jobs) saw to the milk being taken daily to the factory near by. It seemed that an agreement had been reached between the baron, the two guards and the foremen that we would be allowed to work amongst the Polish village people, which proved to be a great success, as many of our lads had never worked on the land before. Not only were they happier but the end result proved more rewarding. It also meant that we could be sent off in smaller working parties, with no German guards, apart from an occasional visit during the day.

Potato-picking for many of us became a back-breaking job. A Polish girl and one of us would be allocated a certain length of field in which to gather potatoes, whilst the tractor made a circular tour around the field. For the first few hours, the English boys would help to carry the girls' baskets along with their own, to be emptied into one of the wagons that were placed along the sides of the fields. The girls were not used to this help from the men folk and we tried to explain that in England it was expected for men to help ladies. But as the day wore, on this habit was dropped; it was as much as a man could do to pick up his own basket, and it was beyond our strength to keep up this chivalry for long (despite having much better rations), especially as, before long, the tractor would be round again, to unearth more potatoes. The problem with the tractor coming round too soon was solved by some of the lads, who had done this in previous years. The answer to the problem was to place some large stones in the rows that the path of the tractor would next reach, these choked the plough and it would be out of action for about twenty to thirty minutes, giving us a bit of a break. We made sure that this would not coincide with one of our official breaks, which occurred every so often.

After about three weeks, it was obvious that there were far too many of us for the state farm, as it was getting difficult to allocate daily tasks, therefore, in a matter of days, we were told that our working party would be cut in half, which upset us, as the living and working conditions were good in comparison to what many of us had experienced before.

The choice of the boys to be returned to the main camp in Thorn would rest, we felt, in the hands of the guards and the two Polish foremen. Between us men there were mixed feelings; there were some who favoured going back to the camp at Thorn, leaving a smaller group from which to choose the remainder. I favoured staying, but it was not my decision. However, when the choice was made, I was one of the so-called lucky ones chosen to remain on the farm, as they had obviously selected the shirkers to go back to the camp. Of the twelve of us who remained, we were a very mixed bag, including an Australian, a New Zealander, an Englishman, a Scotsman and myself, a Welshman. The biggest surprise was that the cockney who was with us was chosen to stay; he was a menace and threat to us and himself. Foolishly, he could not hide his objections and feelings about having to help the Fatherland. Inwardly, we all felt the same, but we knew we had no alternative but to carry on. Fortunately, we were left with the same German guard, who was relaxed in his official duties towards us, and from that time on everything changed for the better. We were allowed to mix more closely with all the villagers on our daily tasks. Each morning, when we were all gathered in the farmyard, we would be sent out in small groups, for various duties, with our guard occasionally checking on us, without his rifle, which meant that we were being trusted. Also, it became apparent that each one of us was more or less being adopted by a Polish family, which also benefited the baron and the two foremen, who were having satisfactory work done and with the least amount of trouble.

The family that the New Zealander and I got attached to consisted of a mother, two sons and two daughters. One of the boys was very much older than us but the others were within our age range. Whilst talking to them, we became enlightened as to their status. They had once owned two farms in Krakow, but they had been turned off overnight, along with many others, with only what they stood up in and the few possessions that they were able to carry, leaving behind all their other possessions and their animals for the Nazi system. Like ourselves, they spoke very little German, so we were all helping each other in that respect, especially as the native language (Polish) was strongly forbidden (maybe because we all found it easier to pick up the Polish language).

I had been nominated to be in charge of the camp first aid

kit, which consisted of some bandages, aspirin and such like, issued from the Red Cross, and added to which were a few German ointments. This job came about as I had attended one or two minor accidents around the farm, which earned me the name, from the villagers young and old, of Doctor, and of Sydney or Taffy, to my fellow prisoners.

If we were fortunate to have a Red Cross parcel, especially clothing parcels from home, the contents were usually shared with the Polish people, as they had subsidised our daily food rations with their meagre food ration, by bringing it out to the fields whilst we worked: egg sandwiches or boiled eggs, whatever they could rustle up.

With the potato-picking finally coming to a close, the remaining crops were now being stored in potato clamps, which were piled up and then covered with earth, for use at a later date. With a few weeks to spare before the arrival of the frost and snow, which was needed to harden the root crops such as sugar beet, swedes and carrots, we were kept occupied by threshing the winter crops of wheat and oats. Once again, the machinery was ancient in comparison to what we had in England, and even more ancient compared to what they used in Australia and New Zealand (according to my friends). The threshing machine itself was worked by a long linen belt, driven from a steam powered traction engine. The most unpleasant and dirtiest job in this operation was to be behind the machine, where the straw stalks came out after all the oats or wheat had been extracted into sacks at the other end of the machine. This required quick changes more often than elsewhere, owing to the amount of straw coming through, and it also produced a lot of dust. Owing to the extra energy required to clear the straw continuously coming out, it required constant manpower to keep it clear and to keep everything running smoothly.

Therefore, we invented a method to delay this overdrive; the British did not relish this method, as the Polish girls were feeding the machine and we did not want to involve them in any interference, so we had to do the disrupting. Very quickly, it was arranged either to overload the machine from the top, or fix a belt to come off the driving wheels. Both methods were applied in a very short space of time, by fair means or foul, thereby giving the person behind the machine a breather. The Polish people appreciated all the antics and sabotage we were causing, indirectly, when the coast was clear. It was something they were unable to do, owing to the consequences. They welcomed these disruptions as a form of reprisal for the way they were thrown out of their homes by the Nazi regime. As human beings, it was hard to believe that such brutality existed towards the old folk and children; as fighting soldiers, we expected harsh treatment but it should not have been directed at civilians.

The first sign of winter 1943 was the frost that started to form on the remaining cabbage and sugar beet crops. Once again it was the duty of the baron to get his farm labourers, Polish and ourselves, to raise the crop and dispatch it, some to Germany and a portion to a sugar beet factory some distance away. This meant that we were arranged into small parties, some working alongside the villagers, male and female, uprooting the vegetables and removing the leaves, whilst others were sent to the local railway sidings, to load either sugar beet or cabbages, which had been ordered by the German High Command in Berlin as essential for that period.

Owing to the weather getting colder daily, it was the custom for all the householders to barricade all windows and doors with straw-filled wooden shutters. It was now October and the weather grew more severe every day and, in spite of these weather conditions, we had to continue to convey a full daily quota of the sugar beet and cabbage. It was now drawing to the end of October and it was reminding me of home and of my sister Doreen's birthday on the 29th October. When her day arrived, it was very windy and it was my turn to load the railway wagon, along with several others. My Polish partner and I were detailed to empty the horse-drawn wagon of its load. We had to clear up what had fallen to the floor and then judge how much more the wagon would take, before we would have to close the heavy steel doors. This was because it was far easier to throw straight into the wagon for as long as possible, rather than over the steel doors, which took more effort. Also, we had more opportunity to damage as many crops as we could, by stamping on them and piercing them. Unfortunately, during my close inspection of the wagon, a strong gust of wind released one of the wagon doors and trapped me against the side. All I can remember is hearing a loud human cry. My fellow workers all heard and came running, shouting, "Taffy's had it." Seeing that I was bleeding badly, they all rallied round and the emptied Polish wagon was sent back to camp at a gallop to get more assistance. I found out later that the baron arranged for one of his best coach horses, attached to a wagon filled with straw and blankets, to collect me. I can only vaguely remember returning to camp. With all due respect to the German guards, the baron and his family, they bent over backwards to help me, and they sent transport to fetch the local civilian doctor from the next village. In no time at all, he was by my side and, after a close examination, it appeared that my ribs had penetrated my lung, causing the blood to escape to my mouth. This was obviously what had frightened my fellow countrymen, when they had first picked me up. I also had several broken teeth and a gash under my chin. It was decided between the doctor, the baron and the guards that I would need to stay in bed and off work for one week, having just sips of water; after this, the doctor would call again, to reassess me. It appeared that the whole village had gone into 'half mourning' for me, and they were all praying for Sydney Santitäter (First Aider), that he had a full recovery and could be back amongst them soon. When word got around that I was able to eat solids again, my fellow countrymen also benefited from the extra delicacies that I received from the whole village, such as white bread, eggs, biscuits and other things. True to his word, the doctor paid me a final visit and left instructions for light duties, which everyone made sure were carried out.

I can honestly admit that each and every night, whatever the circumstances, ever since my early childhood, I managed to say a silent prayer. I continued this habit by saying a prayer of thanks for surviving each day, although, on many occasions, this was often very difficult to do, but I kept faithfully to my upbringing. Often my mind would wander towards some of the treatment we had received and how we survived, especially as my parents had prepared far more nourishing food for the family pig than we were given in the camps. Although, I have to admit that the others and I were currently living in luxury, compared with how we had lived and survived up to this time.

Owing to the limited number of daylight hours, the weather conditions deteriorating and heavy snowfalls, we had to curtail outside work and change over to indoor work, such as cleaning out the cattle pens. True to form, I spent my time helping the carpenter to repair the local Polish villagers' homes, including the big house where the baron and his family lived. Mind you, my help in their homes consisted of me handing the tools and wood to the carpenter. Needless to say, the welcome that I was receiving in each homestead was indescribable and I was always privileged to share with them whatever they had to offer, although we ourselves were quite comfortable as things stood, especially as we were being very well catered for, with lots of fresh vegetables.

Each and every one of the families would pour out the same story of how they had been turned out of their own homes and farms and then transported miles away, and left here, at Gut' Delau. I must admit that the work carried out was very limited, as we would invariably sit down and chat, taking things easy for seventy-five percent of the time. This chat would take place with them chatting in their broken German, and we with our broken Polish, and so we entertained ourselves.

With the approach of Christmas, everyone seemed in a joyous mood and, fortunately, we had kept the same old German guard, which was very unusual as they were normally changed on a regular basis. With Christmas over, and having received many extras from the villagers, we all hoped and prayed, including the baron's family and the guard, that by next Christmas (1944) the war would be over and we would all be home. One sad event did occur just before Christmas: the baron and his wife had the misfortune of losing their son, who was serving in the Luftwaffe, but the baron was most thankful that the boy had not died when he was flying over England. It appears that he was on a training flight when he was killed. This upset us because the baron was so considerate to us, and was far more lenient to us, by providing us with the extra food rations. The baron's daughter, who was the eldest and an excellent horsewoman, spoke very good English and was always anxious to improve it by speaking to us at every opportunity, which was quite often because of the way the baron was.

On New Year's Day 1944, we had what was considered to be an 'annual event', a hare shoot on the estate, and this was the second year it had been run at the farm. We were briefed on the procedure and what to expect, and we were anticipating the arrival of eighteen to twenty other landowners and barons from outlying estates. They arrived in all their finery and shooting attire and heavily laden with medals and ribbons of all descriptions, awarded for past achievements. They arrived in very smart coaches drawn by horses, and entered the house, to be entertained by our baron. Sometime after their arrival, they would appear out of doors, having drunk their fill of schnapps, prior to venturing out to the shoot.

While it was daylight, the villagers and us were used as beaters. We spread out across the fields, with the Polish villagers, while the German riflemen lined up, ready to fire. The snow was still thick on the ground and we had to walk miles backwards and forwards across the fields, to beat the hares, when they appeared, into the centre of the field for the riflemen to shoot. We knew that the riflemen were mentally counting their kills and noting their skill, and we jokingly said that they would be presented with another medal by Hitler for it. Although we knew they were mentally counting their kills, an arrangement had been made between the Polish and ourselves, that we would leave the occasional hare buried in the snow, for their use. One of the duties was to put an end to any wounded hares, by using the sticks that we were carrying, and to carry them back to the meeting point. As everyone closed in and brought their poor little victims to be counted, the riflemen would insist that they had shot more hares than had been brought back. We knew this to be true, by about three or four hares, as we had already buried them, to be picked up after dark by the Polish.

Unfortunately, on one counting, a silly misunderstanding took place, which could have ended in disaster. It appears that Rob, the Australian, had dropped down his hares in the usual manner but apparently, instead of putting all the heads together, he put them head to tail; this, of course, upset the Germans. Then, to make matters worse, I arrived a few minutes later, and quite innocently laid down the poor victims in a similar manner. When this happened, there was uproar, but what made matters worse was that the German bellowed and shouted, his face red with rage, "Foolish Englishman." Of course, I responded and called him a square-headed bloody German and, in a flash, I was staring down a double-barrelled shotgun and was trying hard not to show that I was quivering in my boots with fear. Our senior foreman came rushing up, begging for my safety, as I was a good worker and the camp's medical doctor. My fellow countrymen and the villagers were all praying for me as the German was in such a rage and I was still shaking. The situation was calmed but the German obviously understood a lot of English, to act as he did, especially over a very innocent mistake.

During the next few weeks, things carried on much as normal, owing to the very severe cold weather. Fortunately, our mail kept arriving, so, with that, our living conditions and the fresh vegetables, we were reasonably well off. Also, news was filtering through that the war was now running in our favour, with heavy German losses on the Eastern front. Naturally, the news encouraged the Polish people, too.

Unfortunately, one day early in February a bombshell arrived; we were all away from camp, scattered at our various jobs in the fields (except for the cook), when, on our return for lunch, we were informed that we had had a visit from the Gestapo SS. They had rummaged through the billets and all our personal belongings. We now experienced what the Polish people had accounted to us. They had ransacked everything inside and out, leaving a trail of destruction. We also noticed that some of our things were missing, such as soap, toothpaste and toothbrushes, sent either from home or from the Red Cross. Most of our clothes, being khaki, were not touched, but my medical chest, which had been made for us by a local carpenter, was stripped of all the British aspirin and ointments.

According to the cook, who was present, the sole purpose of the visit was to look for a wireless or any escape material. In that respect, I am afraid their efforts were all in vain, as we were always kept well informed and up to date with events by our locals.

A few days after this visit, we had bad news about our old 'Daddy', the German guard. We got on really well with him, especially as we had some control over him by (rightly) making him cups of tea and Ovaltine and giving him cigarettes. He therefore turned a blind eye to many of our benefits, and accepted our excuses for calling at the local family homes for a borrowed tool or some such thing. The shock that awaited us was huge. When we got back from work, he was waiting to tell us himself, with much sorrow, that since the Gestapo visit, he was to be relieved of his duties. Obviously we, too, were very upset. The old boy's departure, for him and us, was very emotional, especially as we had had so much of our own way (bar complete freedom), and he thanked us for our consideration.

His replacement was a (much hated) younger SS German, and we were soon to realise that it was certain that things would drastically change, and not for the better. From our first meeting, we all sensed that he was up to no good and that we would have to tread very cautiously. Right from his maiden speech and his warnings, we knew he would be trigger-happy and we would have to watch our step. Our instinct proved right in a very short while. He was going to do everything by the book, and intended to carry out his duties to the letter. He was a full bloodied HITLER'S MAN and everything he did was for the Fatherland.

All the connections with the civilian population were brought to an abrupt end. All of us were shocked, when we learnt the fate of the little stray dog that we all, both the locals and us, idolised (but especially the lad from Salford, Manchester, who was his 'owner and trainer'). Whilst we were toiling in the fields, the German guard had brutally shot him, using two or three rounds of ammunition. On our return to camp, we found out what had happened, and we buried the little fellow by the entrance of the village church, which was only an arm's length from our front gate. Like all other churches, it had been robbed of everything of value, and the German command had now forbidden its use for any religious services.

This little village of Gut' Delau was now full of fear, with everyone, civilians and Prisoners of War, on tenterhooks. It was not known where the order came from, but each night, with the exception of two men, all our uniforms including our boots were collected, taken away from us, stored in the church overnight and collected the following morning by the two men who had been allowed to retain their clothes. This, being the middle of winter in Poland, was no joke. The SS man's reason was that we would attempt to escape, which was utterly impossible, with the weather conditions at this time of the year and with our nearest sea port being Danzig, which was approximately one hundred kilometres away. Even our rations were closely watched, and so everyday became a nightmare, with our lives hanging in the balance. This situation carried on for weeks, and each night, and I am sure the same was true of my fellow comrades, we prayed thankfully for surviving another day.

This German guard regularly demanded aspirin and other things from my first aid chest, so much so that he was seriously depleting my supply of everything, no doubt to ease whatever his problem was. A handful of us got together in confidence and decided to bluff our way, when it came to the medicine. When one of his very many requests came through, one of us would scrape the whitewashed walls into a small glass of water, just enough to colour it, and we would get him to drink it immediately. We did this on more than one occasion, and it helped to preserve our stock.

Although he came to see me for treatment, he also had a great dislike of me, because it appeared that the Polish girl, Ludka, who had been very kind to me, by giving me bits of food and even darning my socks, had refused to meet with him, something he resented. She would not meet him because her family could not bring themselves to forgive the Germans for robbing them of their farm home and belongings in Krakow.

I first became aware of his grudge against me when Ludka cut her foot, and one of the foremen and the daughter of the baron contacted me and asked me to dress her wound, which meant going to her home, along with the baron's daughter, as the guard was elsewhere. We all thought everything was okay to go, but it was not to be; the guard returned unexpectedly and found us doing something he thought we should not have been doing. Thankfully, I had the support of the baron's daughter and the foreman to explain my errand of mercy and the circumstances. Had the guard been armed, I am afraid my number would have been up.

This was not the only incident involving this guard. On another occasion, we all thought this maniac had gone to the railway station, some distance away. We all came happily into lunch, talking and laughing, as we usually did. Civilians and Prisoners of War walked together through the farm entrance, as we normally did before this madman arrived. We parted company, the villagers to go to their homes and we to the camp. As we climbed the wooden steps to our billets, who should come out onto the veranda and make a beeline for me? The one person I did not want to see, our German guard. He had obviously seen Ludka and I walking hand-in-hand, as had some of the others, from the camp window. When they saw his attitude towards me, my fellow countrymen gathered round me. Had he been armed, they swore that Taffy would have suffered the same fate as the little dog.

Even though he saw me as his enemy, he still came to me for his medicine, which I grudgingly gave. By this time, the guard had also got fed up with the routine of removing our clothes every evening, but his attitude towards the enemy prisoners was still felt very strongly.

During his time with us, which was approximately two months, we had only one delivery of Red Cross parcels. These parcels usually arrived after dark, so an idea was suggested that we would fake a Red Cross parcel, to tempt 'his Lordship' with. The original plan was to fill the parcel with shit, but thanks to the level headedness of a few of us, we managed to get that stopped. The two who had wanted to do this were an Irishman and a cockney, and they were a problem to us all. Not only were their actions and attitudes causing us much concern, on more than one occasion, they failed to realise that we were still Prisoners of War; which we sometimes tended to forget because we had previously been very lucky in our guards. Hopefully, this one would not be with us very much longer as each day we feared for our lives, with his attitude towards us, and the consequences could be bad. Anyway, we emptied a parcel of its contents, filled it with straw, replaced the packing and tied it up identically to how it was when it had been unopened, and then we dropped it back to where the lorry stopped. At a later date, we were informed by the Polish servants of the house that he had picked up the parcel, taken it to his quarters in the mansion and opened it, hoping to enjoy the contents. Apparently, he blew his top about the contents, but there was very little that he could do about it as he should not have had the parcel in the first place, since it was POW property. Unknown to him, his movements had been watched and, therefore, it gave much pleasure to all of us, when we heard of his disappointment in his findings. Knowing full well that he could not take any action against us, because he should not have been in possession of the offending Red Cross parcel, we had the last laugh.

Late spring and early summer 1944. Much to our relief, we had the good news that our SS maniac had left and, on returning to camp, we found a much older German guard as a replacement. Our first impressions were right: we felt we were once again going to be lucky, and in a very short space of time, our instincts proved to be correct. We did go back to our usual bribes, such as a cup of tea and cigarettes when they were available, and very soon he was on our side. To everyone's relief, the civilians and ourselves, we were back to our old routine and working in harmony.

Once again, the ever present topic of the second front was able to be discussed amongst everyone, especially with our guard, as he hated being a soldier as much as we did, and longed to get back home to his wife and family.

Our letters from home and our clothing parcels were arriving quite frequently again, so we had more to share with our Polish friends, this time with the full knowledge of the guard.

Work on the farm, now it was summer, was getting more interesting, after all the monotonous winter jobs, such as stone-picking, opening up potato clamps and sugar beet and leaves for the indoor feeding of cattle. Little groups, sometimes with civilians and other times on our own, were sent to the furthest point of the farmland, with no fear of a guard at anytime. On a few occasions, I was given the opportunity to exercise and ride the huge, heavy stallion, which I thoroughly enjoyed. On one occasion, much to everyone's delight, and I mean everyone's, on our return from working in the fields for our midday break, we were informed that the British army had landed in France. The news had leaked through but we had to wait patiently for the news to be confirmed. The following days kept us all in deep suspense, hoping and praying that the landing had proved successful, as what we were told was very, very brief. Although in suspense, everyone went about their tasks happier than before with the good news from the war front.

After a very warm day of haymaking, it was the usual custom to take the horses into the duck pond outside the camp, and on this particular day, I mounted a fairly young horse and guided him into the water. What actually happened I do not really know, but the next thing I knew, I was thrown headlong into the pond and, for some reason, had the presence of mind to turn onto my side, away from the horse as he, too, tumbled down. We could only conclude that he must have missed his footing and stumbled, and my fellow riders all reckoned that I had had a lucky escape, which I openly admit I did, but the incident did not deter me from enjoying that job.

Our guard turned out to be trumps and we all called him Pops; undoubtedly we had fallen on our feet, as he was a gem. He never interfered with us at all, apart from opening us up in the mornings and locking us in at night. Often, he would sit with us at night time, comparing photographs of his family and ours, and he appreciated our behaviour, that was making life so much easier for him. In one respect, we were being very naughty, as we reverted to old habits (stopped by the maniac), and a few of us ventured out after being locked up, by removing the bars from the window and dropping into the cowshed below. We were then able to call on our Polish families nightly for a little entertainment, such as dancing and a sip of schnapps. Also, as a precaution, the villagers would arrange to post sentries outside, in case we had a raid by Polish collaborators. Unfortunately, on one occasion, the sentries slipped up as a raid was made on the village and, along with three or four others, Bobby, the New Zealander, and I were in the house that they raided, but fortunately, they went upstairs to the next floor to search, therefore, we were smuggled out from the bottom floor and into the gardens behind. We were eventually given the signal that all was clear to return and, as usual, we ran some distance, under cover, separately, as a precaution. On our arrival back, we found that the others had also been hurriedly smuggled out and were safe. Had any of us been caught, the consequences would have been too unbearable to even think about, for ourselves, the civilians and our German guard, so it was decided not to venture out again, for everyone's sake.

We were now approaching autumn, and with the pieces of war news we were getting through regarding our advancement in France and on the Eastern front, our thoughts turned to home and making a Union flag, but, fortunately, we did not proceed as we had another visit from the Gestapo and SS. It was during our absence that they called upon us. Even the baron and German guard were disgusted and ashamed at the turmoil and state they left behind them of our belongings, with many items missing. To us all, civilians and ourselves, it was obvious that the signs of defeat were showing; even Pop, our guard, was aware of this and was pleased that things were going in our favour.

As usual, the harvest was gathered in, at least what was left after the amount that was transported into Germany, and after we had done our usual sabotaging of the crops whilst loading them into the railway wagons. The crops that were left, such as potatoes, carrots, swedes and sugar beet, were stacked in the open fields and covered over with earth (which was called clamped), for winter storage; even the sugar beet leaves and other leaves were saved for animal fodder. It was surprising how well they kept during the winter months.

The civilians were preoccupied with boarding up all their windows and doorways with straw, in preparation for the severe winter weather, which arrives in early November. We were all optimistic and feeling more light-hearted with the war news, sure that this would be the last winter for them and us in such conditions; they were more or less prisoners like us. Owing to the days being so short of daylight, we were kept occupied around the farm, with threshing etc. Although our Red Cross parcels seemed to have ceased, mail from home came fairly regularly, with news from parents and girlfriends, some broken romances, happy and sad news.

Christmas in Delau was again with us. This would be our second Christmas here at the farm, which was a blessing in itself, compared to what we suffered in the earlier years, of 1940, 1941 and 1942. At least we had warmth and a comfortable billet, with plenty of logs for fires and hot water. A few weeks before Christmas, as previously, we were taken some kilometres away, to dig up huge tree roots and to do replanting for a new forest. We really enjoyed this as it was a change from farm work. Around this festive time, a handful of us did break our pledge and venture out before we were locked up for the night, as the civilians wanted us to celebrate the coming Christmas. I remember quite distinctly being first back outside the camp and waiting for the arrival of Bobby. I had already undone the barbed wire, ready to crawl in, when I decided to wait a few minutes extra, so we could crawl in together. I propped myself leisurely against the wall and gate post and, lo and behold, who should come round the corner? Not Bobby, but Pop, the guard! I do not know who was surprised the most, him or me.

He asked me what I was doing there and I told him I had come out for fresh air and a breather, so he opened the gate and we went in together. My concern now was Bobby, but it appears that Bobby had spotted him as he was coming down to the camp and had laid low, guessing that Pop had come to lock up earlier than usual. As we all chatted there, Bobby walked in, adjusting his trousers as normal, and there were no questions asked, and he had replaced the wire before joining us.

As usual, the village folk supplied us with extra fancies over Christmas, such as cakes, biscuits and egg sandwiches from their small rations, and they appreciated what we could give them, when we received parcels from home, which now was not very often. The villagers, like us, were looking forward to January 1st and the annual feast.

New Year's Day 1945 was the annual get together for the beating for the house shoot by the local German gentry, with the same faces as the previous year. Although we all knew that things were not going too well for the Germans in the war, as they had suffered heavy losses in Russia the previous winter, and the British were advancing so well, their personal opinion was still the same, that they would be able to win. The same procedure occurred as the previous year, and, with our Polish friends, we managed to save a few rabbits for ourselves.

Due to the normal severe weather conditions in Poland, with temperatures well below zero, we were confined mostly to indoor work, apart from occasionally having to open up a clamp of potatoes and carrots for the baron's use and ours. Also, we got the sugar beet and leaves for the animals. This meant that just a few boys had to go out, two or three times a week, with the Polish driver, to load up the wagon. The rest of us would be occupied all around the farmyard, while we waited for the arrival of the wagon, so that we could unload it, which was much warmer work, in the shelter of the buildings, than out on the fields.

Daily, the Poles would inform us that the Russians were making good headway towards us and it would only be a matter of time before they would be with us. Fortunately, everybody played it cool and carried on normally.

Towards the middle of January, we were urgently woken up in the early hours of the morning by the guard, told to dress immediately and take with us only what we could carry. We were going to be moving out at daybreak, destination unknown. From past experience, we gathered together as much food as we had, extra clothing and blankets. Anything that was surplus we left behind, to be distributed to the Polish families, and I am sure that they would appreciate all they received.

At daybreak, we left the camp for the last time. Outside, all the villagers, young and old, had gathered to wish us farewell. I don't think there was a dry eye amongst them or us. Much to our surprise, the baron had supplied us with one wagon and two of the best horses on the estate, with a driver to carry our few possessions for the first kilometres. Also under the layer of straw was a young piglet that had been killed, but, owing to the suddenness of our departure, it was impossible to roast. Much to our disappointment, we were at a loss about what to do with it.

Before making our final farewell, we all glanced around the farmyard, where stood a half empty wagon of sugar beet leaves that another lad and I had been unloading the previous afternoon, only a few hours earlier, not realising then that it was to be my last job on the farm. Even the baron and his family stood in the background to wish us farewell. I must confess that our sudden departure made us all very downhearted. Our poor guard did not know where our destination was to be. He was only told to make for such and such a point.

We set off into high snow drifts and easterly winds. Fortunately, we had no knowledge of what was ahead of us. Over the following six weeks, we covered approximately between fifteen to sixteen miles a day, in biting winds and snow, with temperatures well below freezing. Occasionally, we were joined by other British prisoners, making our column longer.

Each and every day consisted of the same thing, with us starting off at daybreak. We kept struggling on, with no one knowing our destination or where we would be sleeping that night, and our only consolation was hearing the Russian artillery fire getting closer and closer.

We slept where we could, finding shelter in various places, such as old barns or any outbuildings, and it was a case of first in nabbing the best of the shelter, so it meant getting to the front of the column. On more than one occasion, I woke up covered in snow.

These conditions were the opposite extreme to what we had experienced marching through France in 1940, in intense heat. It was now bitterly cold, with a freezing east wind that was taking its toll on fellow comrades, who were falling by the wayside and freezing. Soon we were without food and with little left of what we had carried away with us. Even our own original party had got smaller.

As bad as things were, our old German guard looked out for us each night, even though the Germans, too, were now short of food and similar to us. A catastrophe occurred one night, when Jock and I were sleeping next to each other. My Red Cross blanket was taken from us and we were left with only Jock's small, single blanket between us. Although our boots were frozen to our feet, it would have been very unwise to remove them and leave them unattended; the only consolation was that we could change our socks and replace the boots straight away.

By now the food had more or less come to an end and it was a case of the strongest surviving. We had been marching for about three weeks in the sub zero temperatures, and to stop or even stumble would have been fatal. Over some of the previous days, many of our comrades had fallen by the wayside and had been just left to freeze to death, as we were too weak to assist them in anyway. Many of the German guards, with good humane intentions, shot them where they lay, so as to prevent further suffering, which we all felt was the best thing to do.

Over the following days, the whole column was getting smaller and smaller, and as each night fell, it showed how our numbers were dwindling. One day, we were ordered to stop and gather together, and, much to our surprise, a high ranking German officer and his fellow staff came along. He had come to address us after they had found the bodies of our lads along the wayside and discovered that they had been shot in the head.

Although he understood the reason and the conditions that this was carried out in, he ordered it to be stopped immediately, as the Russians were so close behind us. In a matter of days, we could be their prisoners, and they would be tempted to do likewise with us, so we did not slow them down. The best he could do for us and his fellow countrymen was to keep us pressing on, to get to Germany or some Prisoner of War camp along the way.

To the best of my recollection, I calculated that it was about the second Sunday in February 1945, and we had now been marching for approximately one month, when the column was brought to a halt in an isolated village, due to a heavy blizzard, which it was utterly impossible to travel through. It was obvious that we all appreciated the short break and we sorted out whatever shelter was available. After some time, we were ordered to start marching again. Although it was still snowing heavily, we felt much better and able to brave the conditions. The snow was now much deeper and it was only a short distance from where we had rested when we came across two young women and a young child trudging along, fighting the severe elements, like ourselves. Feeling sorry for them, I gathered that they were Polish refugees or German, as I spoke to them in both languages. I offered to carry the child, which they immediately handed over. I gave Victor my shoulder bag, which now consisted of my razor, wash things, one or two pairs of socks and photographs, for safe-keeping. I explained to Pop, our old German guard, what I had done and his response was that I was crazy. I also explained that I would leave the child in the first house that we came across. The two girls also knew this and fully agreed with me. Fortunately for me, we had only gone a few kilometres, when I spotted a farm house some distance from the roadway. Trying to be true to my promise, I knew that I would have to get to that house, knowing only too well that, if I took it upon myself to venture across the field, I could face certain death from one of the German guards, who may think that I was trying to escape, and it would be very obvious, as my footprints would be highly visible. Therefore, as a precautionary measure, I waited for Pop, our German guard, to catch us up and I explained to him what I intended doing. He fully agreed to me taking and leaving the child at the farm house, and, being the good person that he was, he stood at the roadside, safeguarding my rear during the journey, which was approximately four hundred to five hundred yards. With my precious load, I finally reached the house, and I can well remember kicking heavily against the front door. It was eventually answered by an elderly couple. I explained to them that I was an England Prisoner of War (they knew us as England rather than English), and that I had with me a young child, and that the two young girls would follow later, and call for the child. I was warmly welcomed indoors, where I found two or three other people huddled around a circular stove. After they had relieved me of the child, I immediately placed my bare arms onto the top of the stove, as they were completely numb from carrying the child that distance.

Thanking them for their help, I took my leave and returned to where Victor and the guard were waiting for me. As soon as I got back, Victor slammed a handful of snow into my face, as apparently it had been frostbitten. I didn't realise then, but my hands and feet had also been severely frostbitten. Continuing marching and still struggling on through the blizzard, I tried to get the circulation going in my arms.

For the next two or three days, we battled along under terrible arctic conditions, with our numbers still getting smaller and smaller. Nightfall became a tremendous worry; we never knew what kind of shelter we would have. Invariably, everything was getting far worse, each night and day. There was no food available to anyone. There was a great temptation to pick up the snow to eat, and that would have been fatal as it would have made us even colder.

It was now around the middle of February, and I can well remember a derelict farmyard where Victor and I struggled into one of the stables and were fortunate to have loose straw to bed down in, which felt like a luxury. Later, we were joined by a few others, but our only consideration was to lie down and get some sleep. Not only were we wet and tired, but my face, hands and feet were beginning to show signs of discolouration and, unfortunately, Victor had dropped and lost my belongings, leaving us with nothing and absolutely no reserve to fall back on. What could anyone say, under the circumstances? I can honestly confess that at the end of each day, I thanked God for letting me survive another day. This is something that was very important to me, throughout my four years in captivity, and whatever the circumstances had been during that day, good or bad. After this particular night, spent in semi luxurious conditions, we were preparing to set off on another day's march to the unknown, when Vic and I noticed that a fellow countryman seemed unable to join us. On further investigation, we saw that his body, hands and feet had been frostbitten beyond bearing. There was no alternative but to leave him and a few others behind.

This was now a daily occurrence. Men just gave up fighting the elements and starvation. The outcome could be anyone's guess. Who knew whether the Russians or anyone else would arrive to help them in anyway? This being a daily sight, we got hardened to it; it was now just a case of survival of the fittest. Even the German guards had got fewer in numbers.

To the best of my knowledge, we had been walking in these conditions for roughly six weeks, and, by now, I was getting concerned about the frostbite. Between the discoloration and numbness, my whole body was beginning to flag.

About mid morning, our old German guard told Victor and me that he had heard there was a Prisoner of War camp in the vicinity, but in a different direction to the way we were going. Although Victor and I had been such close comrades to each other all along, I decided, because of being in such a bad condition, that I didn't have anything to lose by venturing out to find this camp. Therefore, I gave Victor the option either to come with me or continue with the remnants of the column, as the Germans by now were also at the end of their tether and couldn't care less. I also passed on the message to some of the others marching close by. Vic decided to carry on, so, wishing Vic and Pop, our old German guard, goodbye and a safe journey home, because I was not in a position to shake hands, I parted company with them. They went straight on, and about ten or so of us changed direction and went down the left hand road. With the temperatures far below freezing and with it snowing heavily, we travelled a fair few kilometres and I was beginning to wonder if I had mistaken the instructions and missed the camp that was supposed to be in the vicinity. Not only was the weather deteriorating, but our morale was getting very, very low, wondering if we had made the right decision. We were very much on our own, all British lads, with no German guards to protect us.

Eventually, much to everyone's relief, we could see in the distance some huts, and we sincerely hoped and prayed that we could at least have shelter for the night. Regaining some hidden strength, we managed to get into the compound just when daylight was fading. We were only too pleased to get this far and made a beeline for the nearest door. Much to our surprise and fright, on entering the room, we came face to face with a small group of soldiers. Although we were dressed in our battledress, they were in sub headdresses, with heavy beards and very dark skin, difficult to see properly, due to the lack of electricity. It is hard to say who was the most scared, them or us, as we looked nothing like British soldiers, being so wet, cold and muffled up, to try to keep warm. We had great difficulty in explaining who and what we were. Eventually, we understood that they were subs serving in the British army, and it was obvious that our visit was not very welcomed. They were huddled together in groups, and we managed to understand that there was another camp, consisting of French soldiers, some distance away. So, for everyone's sake, we were only too pleased to turn our backs on them; each and every one of us was scared of staying with such hard and cruel looking men.

Needless to say, we managed to find a little bit more of that extra strength and made a getaway that was as quick as possible. True to what they had told us, we did eventually reach a French camp. Luckily, when we arrived there, we were greeted far more warmly, as by now night had fallen. With the few improvised lights that they had, we could see that the living conditions were quite good and it was obvious that they had received regular parcels from home. They were also far better dressed than we were; not having had to march, they had managed to maintain a very good bodily appearance.

Realising the poor condition that we were in, they soon made bed spaces for us to lie down in that night, which was greatly appreciated, especially as it was warm and dry. It was an opportunity for me to remove my boots for the first time in five weeks. We all slept very soundly that night and in the morning, when I crawled out from my bottom bunk, we were flabbergasted at the condition of my face and hands from the frostbite. It appeared that I was the only one in this state; the others had managed to avoid frostbite. Their kindness towards me was beyond price, they even washed and shaved part of my face and trimmed my hair. Luxury seemed to have returned, especially with the delivery of coffee and bread for breakfast. My face and hands were then dressed, to the best of their ability and under the difficult circumstances. When I think back to May 1940, and the French woman who slammed a door in my face when I asked if she would heat up a tin of soup for my breakfast, my opinion of the French, very low then, now went up a great deal.

During the course of the morning, we were asked by the

French about whether we were going to stay or move on. The weather conditions were still bad and it was up to us. I was prepared to move on but was not in any fit state to decide for myself so I left it to the others to make the decision, and it was decided that we would carry on, whatever the consequences. Before leaving, we thanked the French soldiers most sincerely for our overnight stay and care.

The French soldiers had told us about an American camp that was somewhere in the vicinity, and we headed off in that direction. Fortunately, their information was correct and we eventually arrived at a seemingly deserted American camp, on the borders of Poland and Germany. I say seemingly deserted, as we were welcomed by a small group of roughly two dozen or so of our own countrymen, including a Welsh guardsman, Lawrence, who was from Cardiff and who served in the same battalion as me.

Immediately I was given VIP treatment and whisked off to be stripped and put into a bed, which was complete with the ultimate luxury of white sheets and pillows. How the American soldiers had lived, in comparison to us. This time, having been undressed and washed properly, I was given a meal of American spam, biscuits and plenty of hot milk, even though it was the powdered variety, which was a luxury in itself.

I was then kitted out with all new American clothing, which was hard for me to comprehend, after the previous six weeks of hell.

My only regret in all this was that my Scottish friend, Victor, had not joined me in my decision but had carried on with the column, under the protection of a few guards.

Lawrence, the Welsh guard, with others, appeared at my bedside with a young medical officer, who immediately took it upon himself to treat my frostbite. In the beginning, he was pessimistic about the bad condition of my hands and fingers, and he feared the worst. There was one small consolation, which was that when I placed my hands on the stove, after carrying the little child, my circulation was numb and the stove caused some blistering, which seems to have restored a little bit of the circulation, which was a good sign. The doctor and I would have to wait and see what the end result would be of his dry dressings and his advice to move my finger joints as much as possible.

A morning or two after our arrival at the camp, I was woken by Lawrence playing a musical instrument to the tune of our regimental march: 'Men of Harlech' and also 'Rising of the Lark'. When I asked why he was playing this, he explained that it was March 1st, 1945, St David's Day. That was the first confirmation of a date that I had had since leaving our farm in Poland, on January 10th, 1945.

Although I was now living in the lap of luxury, the memory of the past few weeks of being in arctic conditions stayed with me, and I was now able to allocate more time to my nightly prayers, to say thank you for my safe passage to this new home.

I was very thankful for the daily attention and nursing that I was receiving from Lawrence and others. I was given priority attention, due to my condition, and daily I was washed, shaved and groomed in bed. Their efforts were being rewarded as the condition of my face, hands and feet was responding to treatment, and the medical officer was pleased every day, when he examined me. He stressed that I must continue with my exercises, and he openly confessed that, even now, he was doubtful that I would ever be able to use my hands again. Inwardly, too, I had some doubts, as I had seen a fellow countryman's hands, some days previously, that had been made useless by frostbite, and this was naturally at the back of my mind.

Daily, we could hear Russian gunfire in the distance but getting nearer. This gave us food for thought as we were entirely on our own, with no German guards to protect us. What would happen if they overran us? They might not realise that we were British squaddies, especially as we were in our makeshift uniforms, a mixture of British and American. Some of the lads had a little knowledge of the Russian language. We were at the mercy of anybody. I believe that some of the lads were in the process of making some Union flags, just to help.

After about ten days, all our hopes were shattered, when we were found by the German High Command and ordered to pack up immediately and leave for the nearest railway station; and so our high living came to an abrupt end. We gathered together as much tinned food and cigarettes as it was possible to carry, which was not a great deal, and left as quickly as possible, owing to the Russian advance. We certainly didn't like this strategy at the time, but it proved to be for the best.

On our arrival at the local railway station, we were herded into cattle trucks, not knowing where we were going; actually, neither did the German guards. The following morning, we were unloaded and marched a few kilometres away, and arrived at a huge camp, which we understood was called 'San-Bostal'. Years later, I gathered that we were somewhere near Belsen, which would have been our final destination. On entering, it was obvious that it had been a huge camp, and each separate compound was wired off. Scattered around us were numerous huts, with American, British, Belgian, French and Russian soldiers, but there seemed to be a reduced number of German guards. Being only a small party, there was no problem with finding our sleeping quarters, which consisted of individual rooms, but there were no bunks available, so it was back to sleeping on the floorboards.

We soon learnt that we were on the flight path of our bombers that passed over nightly, to drop their bombs on the German towns.

My face and hands were still a handicap to me in many things, but I was given unstinting help and assistance from the British and American soldiers, in whose barracks we seem to have landed. As usual, it was best to settle down as quickly as possible in our new surroundings, and, as the old saying goes, 'If you can't beat them, join them,' which, along with the others, I did. I joined the party who were organising a place of worship and although I was limited to what I could do, I did my share.

Fortunately, we had electricity, which caused its own problems; to boil water for a cup of tea, coffee or anything available, we had to be extra careful that the homemade plunger was removed immediately when the water boiled, otherwise it could have blown the fuses. This would cause everyone's electrics to go.

As was the custom, we listened to up-to-date news from the Yanks and others who had been captured after D-day, and they told us all that had happened over the last five years. By coincidence, some of the Americans I had befriended had been stationed in Tenby, West Wales, and they even produced photographs of Caldey Island and the surrounding sights. What surprised me was that their photographs were not destroyed. In 1940, when I was captured, we were ordered to destroy everything.

We had one or two sad skirmishes with the German guards, when, for some reason, they got annoyed or upset and fired their weapons at random. We were to learn that there were a couple of casualties, though, luckily, these incidents were rare.

It was at about this time that I was approached discreetly by a British warrant officer from one of the line regiments, to see if I was interested in purchasing a gent's wrist watch for a very nominal fee. From my past experiences, when leaving the previous camp, I had brought with me a small quantity of American cigarettes. We agreed to the transaction and he handed over a Russian wrist watch that he had purchased from a Russian officer in exchange for a few cigarettes. Obviously, I was quite pleased with my purchase, although I had to rely on others to wind it for me.

A short time later, I was taken to one side, to be asked if I would volunteer for a makeshift working party, to travel to the other end of the camp, which was a fair distance, to be a go-between between our camp and the others. Eventually, I was contacted by two Belgians, who introduced themselves to me unofficially. In a particular room, all types of work was being carried out, officially and unofficially, of, amongst other things, repairing clothes, footwear and furniture; it was quite a hive of activity. The only thing I was expected to do was, when the Germans came in to the room, to sweep up the floors. Other than that small task, I was just sitting around, mostly chatting with the other men, in whatever language I could use. At the beginning and end of the shift, I was given a few finished articles, such as belts, straps and clothing, to hand over to my superiors. This continued daily for about ten to fourteen days, when once again we got a message that many of the British prisoners were to be transferred to another camp. Secretly, I was told that, for my own good, I should be on the party to go. I begged to stay as I was not fully aware of what I had been helping to do, but it fell on deaf ears. It appears that, in recognition of my efforts, between the two sides, the Belgians and the British, they had arranged a farewell surprise for me. That night, after dark, I was collected and taken over to the Belgian quarters, where a small party welcomed me with some food and drink, to celebrate my departure. I was also given a photograph of every Belgian soldier that I had been in contact with. Naturally, I was taken aback by their welcome and hospitality as I hadn't realised what I would be doing, when I volunteered for the job. Apparently, I was taking secret messages between the two camps, hidden in the clothes. After my short stay for my party in the Belgian quarters, I was escorted back safely to my hut.

Many years later, I learned that the Welsh Guards' armoured division, under the command of Major Windsor Lewis, liberated the San-Bostel camp, and he was the officer who, along with other fellow guardsmen, had been captured on the 25th May 1940.

Our departure from San-Bostel started; we had no time to receive or gather any food, and so we travelled light. Where we were going was unknown, as was the usual procedure. We were marched under armed escort to the nearest railway station, and after the normal lengthy wait, our transport eventually arrived; the old familiar cattle trucks were attached to the end of the train. It appeared that this was a troop-carrying train, which made it even more difficult to know where we could possibly be going. I can well remember the date: it was the 31st March 1945, but not the day of the week. There were only a few of us and we were herded into the cattle trucks around mid afternoon, the door and heavy bolt were shut, and we were locked in tight. On this occasion, it was a little bit more luxurious than usual, as they had spread a tiny amount of straw around, with one or two empty boxes for sitting on, if you were lucky. I settled down and continued to read a very soft-cornered, well worn paperback, which I had been given at some point. It was a very appropriate book: *How Green Was my Valley,* by Richard Llewellyn. Unfortunately, my hands were still heavily bandaged, but it was a case of managing the best I could, as my present fellow travellers did not understand my predicament; they were all strangers to me.

As was to be expected, our journey started and we had travelled some distance, when we had the sudden stop that signalled that we had arrived somewhere, and we were shunted back into the sidings. We were not removed from the train, and realised that night had fallen. We lay down, to get as much sleep as possible. Inwardly, we all guessed why we had stopped; it was not because we had reached our final destination, but because this was a troop train and it had to stop, to avoid being detected by our aircraft going overhead, as it would be a sure target.

Long after daybreak, we were still locked in and none the wiser about what was going on, or our whereabouts; therefore, like the others, I carried on reading, whilst some talked or slept. We all joked about it being 1st April 1945 and, therefore, April Fools' Day, and we were all locked up in a cattle truck, far away from home. We had to act humorous to keep up our morale; otherwise, we would soon have cracked. Midmorning we came to another abrupt halt and were again shunted into sidings. We could hear sirens in the distance and, in a very short space of time, we had a warm and loud reception as some Yankee planes began bombing and strafing around us. Although we were overjoyed at their appearance, we were not in a position to welcome them. In fact, we were praying that someone would remember about us, locked away and helpless.

After what seemed like an eternity, we eventually heard the bolts being released and the German who opened the door shouting at us to make for the best shelter we could find. Needless to say, the others and I were most thankful to this kind-hearted and thoughtful German soldier for releasing us. Eventually, things cooled down and the raid was over, their task completed. They had made a jolly good mess of our surroundings and flattened everything. It was fairly obvious that the Americans had had news of the troop movement and were given the job of stopping it.

After a short while, we were all gathered back together and informed by our guards that we were heading for a camp in Falling-Bostel, which was near Bremen, between Hanover and Hamburg. If an opportunity like this had occurred years ago, it would have been a glorious chance to escape, but now we were not physically fit enough, and because of the way the war was now going, it would have been foolish to try; we could have been shot if we had tried.

We were transported to our new destination. It seemed like only a few hours until we reached the camp at Falling-Bostel and we were thankful to have survived another dangerous situation. I remember the train stopping at a tiny halt, and us having to march just a few kilometres to the camp.

My first impressions of this camp were that, at one time, it had been a huge mixed camp, which was opposite a large warehouse and a few scattered dwellings. It seemed to be understaffed but the guards who were there were of the older generation of German guards. The procedure for our admittance to this camp was very relaxed, compared to what I was accustomed to in the other camps. Once inside, we were left more or less to our own devices.

Later, a few of us were directed to an outbuilding, which did not have any beds or bunks, the only sleeping place was once again, as 1940, on Mother Nature's earth. Fortunately, the weather was warm and so we just sat down and carried on as best as possible, something I had experienced many times before.

Food and drink seemed not to be forthcoming from the Germans so we had to rely upon what little amount of food we had brought with us. Needless to say, tempers were short and thieving was prominent. During the next couple of days, news filtered through that a quantity of Polish Red Cross parcels had been found. I was very surprised to hear that the Red Cross parcels were only for the Poles. Being they were for the Polish soldiers, I was persuaded by one or two fellow countrymen, as I could speak a little bit of Polish, to join the queue and pretend that I had Polish connections. I succeeded in bluffing my way through the short interview and I was rewarded with a parcel, much to everyone's delight, although in the years that followed, I often felt guilty, especially as I used my mother's date of death. Starvation knows no bounds. As usual, the contents, once opened, were shared amongst us.

My next good fortune was that, having attached myself to take the sick parade every morning and evening in the RAF compound, some hundreds of yards away, I was given a special pass from the German camp commandant, which I still have to this day, and it gave me permission to enter other compounds.

One of our greatest delights, day and night, was seeing the Yanks flying over during the day, and our own lads flying over at night, on their way to bomb the German cities and on their way back to England. Many of them would dip their wings as they flew over, indicating that they were well aware of our whereabouts.

Very suddenly, one day, I was told that I was wanted at a nearby, make-shift sick bay. Wishing to oblige, I made use of my pass and casually passed through the sentries, who by this time were quite familiar with all my comings and goings. Arriving at the sick bay and not knowing what to expect, I was taken aback to see my old Scottish pal, Vic Oliver of the Black Watch, who I had last seen when we parted company in February, when he decided to follow the column, whilst I and a few others found the American hospital.

Vic was barely recognisable. Not only was he a very sick man, but his shirt and clothing had not been changed since we started off on the march in early January. After greeting him, he was too feeble to respond, I immediately removed his shirt and underwear and replaced them with my own American shirts and clothing, as I knew I had left replacements back in the billet. For this kindness, which seemed to me the right thing to do, a huge cheer and clap arose from the fellow inmates, who consisted of mostly RAF boys. Not to exert him too much, I quickly went away, and returned to share what little food I had with me, left over from the Polish parcels. Not that they were very much use to poor Vic, as he did not have the strength to eat very much.

My very few visits were cut short owing to sniper fire coming from the retreating German army. We were all ordered to keep away from the main entrances of the camp, for our own safety. It was becoming obvious that our advancing troops were very near at hand, as machine gun and rifle fire was getting closer and closer. The rumours were getting stronger that British troops were in the vicinity.

Around the second Monday in April, I was asked to take half a dozen or so sick comrades down to the Medical Officer for the usual check-up and, when I was half way there, a cry went up, "They are here at the front gates." My sick comrades made a miraculous recovery and they just vanished. I carried on to the Medical Officer, to tell him that all those with ailments had suddenly recovered. On my way back, the German guard, an elderly man, handed me his rifle. I unloaded the few rounds of ammunition left in the gun, and we walked steadily back together. I can remember him telling me that he was now the prisoner and I was the guard, but he was thankful to be relieved of his duties.

The British prisoners were too busy tearing down the barbed wire entanglements to notice him and me casually walking together. I learnt that it was a Welsh regiment who were liberating us, and remembering my own experience in 1940, when I was taken prisoner, I did likewise to this old German soldier. I had no intention of searching him or depriving him of anything and just handed him over to an NCO, and when he asked me what he should do with him, I replied, "Look after him, he is one of the best."

Obviously the advancing troops were overjoyed at releasing us and were busy handing out cigarettes and things, while others were searching and combing out the Germans, who were trying to take cover. The military police were trying hard to control us, but it was natural that everyone wanted to get out. Finally, they prevailed, as we were still under military law, which had to be obeyed.

We were restricted to the camp compound, while the advancing troops searched all the surrounding areas, and we were warned that the Hitler Youth movement was very strong and treacherous in the area, and its members were known to shoot soldiers in the back.

In a matter of hours, we had an abundance of tea and food, which was shared with the advancing troops. Also a contingent of RAMC orderlies arrived with the delousing equipment, which we were all thoroughly showered with.

In the meantime, we were addressed by the British Officers and photographed by the press photographers, who enlightened us as to exactly how the war was progressing and said that as soon as transport was available, we would be returned back to dear old Blighty, but for our own safety, we were warned not to wander away from the camp.

Eventually, I befriended a transport driver and a fellow comrade from the Newport Monmouthshire area in Wales, who invited me to join them on their journeys back and forth with replacement food and ammunition, which I enjoyed immensely, travelling between the white-taped clear areas.

Unfortunately, on the last short trip in semi-darkness, someone had changed the signposts, which could have led us back into enemy hands on our return trip. Luckily, this was spotted in time by the driver, who realised that something was wrong; he immediately reversed back some distance and picked up the right direction, much to everyone's relief. I was certainly not prepared to take on another stretch of imprisonment, having been brought back to safety, so I wished them God speed and good luck for the future, but did not go with them again. At a much later date, one of this crew called in at Oliver's footwear branch, where I worked in Newport, Monmouthshire, to see me, but unfortunately, I was away on relief. This would have been sometime in 1946.

Monday night, needless to say, there was very little sleep in the camp and, unknown to me and many others, it would be our first night of freedom and our last night at Falling-Bostel, on our Mother Earth bed space.

Daybreak found us all still lively and full of the joys of spring and with plenty to eat, drink and smoke. By midmorning, we were informed that a small contingent would be leaving, to go to a nearby landing strip, to be taken on our way home.

Mid afternoon, we were loaded onto troop carriers and taken to the nearest landing strip, which was many miles away, in the German countryside. We passed lots of advancing troops, who all cheerfully waved us home, shouting, "Bon Voyage." I found a strange contrast in the behaviour and feelings of the advancing, conquering troops, to the downhearted feelings as a retreating army in May 1940. On two or three occasions our cheerful convoy came to a halt, to give us a break. The reception of the local people showed that they were as thankful as we were that the war was drawing to an end, and they were most thankful that British troops had passed through their villages, and not the Russians.

Eventually, we arrived at what was a temporary, makeshift air strip, still somewhere in Germany, and it appeared that we were the first batch of POWs to arrive there. We were a strange mixture of army and RAF personnel. After we had all been unloaded, we were gathered together and it was explained that we would be sleeping under canvas until flights could be arranged to take us home. At the moment, the planes and crews were tied up with bringing in troops and provisions for the advancing army, which we fully understood. In the meantime, we were given plenty of food and tea, enough to satisfy us all. Along with two or three others, I was allocated space in an NCO's tent. Needless to say, it was quite luxurious accommodation and it was great to know that we were sleeping safe and sound with our own countrymen.

Serving personnel on the site were delighted and proud to bring us up to date about what had happened over the last five years and also what to expect when we arrived in London and elsewhere, due to the Blitz, the doodlebugs and the terrible damage that was caused to civilians and property.

We were surrounded by young men, soldiers and airmen, who must have been still in school when I left England in 1940. They now had new fighting equipment, uniforms for combat, and the organisation throughout the fighting front had changed completely. All the men had very high morale, as each day brought more news of our advancing troops conquering new areas. What a difference from when we were in retreat and the Germans had the best of everything. It seemed now that, in 1939/40 we were trained and equipped in methods that were similar to those of 1914–18, whereas the Germans were trained and equipped to a much higher standard than us. Along with many fellow prisoners, I often wondered how they were allowed that level of preparation without us finding out about it.

On the Wednesday, this was the third day after we had been released, we were gathered together to be told that there was a great possibility of us being flown home to England that day. This turned out to be true. In the early afternoon, returning troop carriers arrived, but it was explained that some would land in Belgium or France, whilst others would go straight on to England.

Under orders, we were split into different groups before marching to the waiting aircraft. My group were taken onto a plane, which was scary for many of us, as it was our first experience of flying. Naturally, the size of the plane was surprising and more so the interior, as it had previously been carrying paratroopers and various other troops. I was the last to enter the plane. As each man entered he was instructed to sit on the floor. By the time I got on, my sitting place was next to the door, but I was assured that it would not open until we had safely landed.

The crew came along to introduce themselves to us, and it appeared that they were all Canadian. It was giving them great pleasure to take us on our first stage home, after so many years. The air hostess was there, to give us instructions on what to do and what not to do should an emergency arise, and explain about air sickness that could occur, especially after two days on full British rations.

Not long after take off, we got the great news that we were going straight to England, although our destination was not certain, but they thought it would be somewhere in Oxfordshire. Also during our flight, each man was invited to the flight deck, for an aerial view. When I had my go, I had the pleasure of seeing, for the first time ever, the white cliffs of Dover. Shortly after this, we were told by the WAAF air hostess that we were approaching Oxfordshire, and the pilot very smoothly landed the plane, to place us once again on English soil and safety.

Being the last man on, I had the advantage of being the first man off the plane; and we were all greeted by a crowd of WAAF Auxiliary Service and the Red Cross, who escorted us from the steps of the plane straight to one of the aircraft hangers, where a number of tables were laid out with white tablecloths and plenty of food of all descriptions and the traditional English tea. It became obvious, during the course of the meal, that we were all overwhelmed by the spread and the reception. This was the reality of things we had talked and dreamt about, when we were really hungry and had often woken up disappointed.

After this, we were briefed about what our future arrangements were going to be and were issued with one postcard each, to send to home, to inform our families that we were back in England. It had been four years and eleven months since I had left dear old Blighty.

We were then taken for a complete change of clothing, although much of mine was still quite new and American. I imagine that it was all taken and destroyed, although I did manage to keep my shirt and American hand towels, which I had taken from the American hospital. Unfortunately, the British uniform I had been given was not too good a fit and, at a later date, my sister had to alter it completely. Also, they were unable to supply me with Welsh Guards' shoulder numerals, and I had to make do with Royal Armoured Division ones instead, along with a black beret. The explanation I was given was that my battalion had been converted into a tank regiment. Needless to say, I changed them all as soon as possible, when I arrived home.

On that first night on British soil, many of the lads were sleeping between white sheets for the first time in years, but for me it was not such a novelty, as I had slept between white sheets in the American hospital, back in March. We were not allowed to leave camp but the NAAFI did a roaring trade, even though we were penniless. During the course of the evening everything was free, including the entertainment. Mind you, our cat calls were not quite as expected, as we had been accustomed to various extra phrases over the last five years, some of which are far from repeatable.

After a trouble free, comfortable, but very short night, we were given a hearty breakfast, like the ones we had dreamt of on many occasions when we were very hungry.

Following this, we were brought up to date with the current life in England, such as rationing, and were given various ration books and coupons to take home, all of which we had no knowledge of. We were also issued with railway tokens, a pass and English money, along with, most importantly, six weeks leave.

We were transported to the nearest railway station and left to our own devices to find our way home. My own aim was to head for Paddington railway station, in London. This was more difficult than it sounds, as the names of the stations had been removed during the war. We found it all very amusing, en route to London.

At each station, our party was getting smaller, as many of the lads lived in the vicinity or had connections where they could go.

By the time we arrived in Paddington, there were only

half a dozen of us heading for Wales. It was getting dusk and, on enquiring, we were informed that the next train heading for Cardiff would be the mail and milk train that was leaving around midnight, and it would be taking the longer route, via Gloucester, which was the least of our worries.

On our way to Paddington, we had been surprised and appalled by the sight of all the damage caused by the bombing that had occurred during our absence. Although we had been told by the Germans that they had been heavily bombing England, we thought it was war propaganda, but we now realised it had been true.

Once we had boarded the Cardiff train, we all stretched out in the compartments and tried to catch up on as much sleep as possible, as we had had very little sleep since our release. Although, sleep was sometimes hard, as we often thought that, when we woke up, the entire rescue would have been a dream and we would still be in Germany, under Nazi rule.

On arrival at Cardiff Central, which was still in semi-darkness, two or three of the others and I had to find our way to Cardiff's Queen Street station, to take a train for the Valleys. Still carrying my small parcel containing the remnants of my American clothing, which I had held back, and a German helmet, which I had picked up on my final journey to the airport (later used as a flowerpot by my sister Doreen,), we strolled back through the streets of Cardiff and were amazed at the sand-bagged buildings and other precautions. We saw so many changes as we were on our way to the station.

Somewhere along the route, we came upon a mobile Salvation Army café and they provided us with large mugs of tea, sandwiches and a hearty welcome, when they found out who we were.

Eventually, we arrived at Queen Street station, where we had some time to wait for the first train to leave for Aberdare. This was annoying because I would need to change at Pontypridd. This, however, was the least of my worries, as I was returning home with no mother to greet me, just my father and sister.

Duly arriving at Aberaman railway station, at about 6 o'clock in the morning, I was the only passenger getting out there. I automatically showed my railway pass to the only porter on duty, which was a natural thing to do, but before arriving at the way out, he came running after me, calling my name and apologising for not recognising me as I was descending from the railway carriage.

Since my departure, he had been employed by the Great Western Railway. Prior to that, he had been a collier and was a staunch member of the Welsh Baptist Chapel which I had attended, and he had often reprimanded my friends and me for being naughty and misbehaving in chapel (just boys fooling about).

I then made my way home, taking the same route I had taken five years and five months earlier, along with my mother and father, as they walked me to the station to join the Welsh Guards. For them, it was a very serious occasion as they knew the possible consequences, but to me, at twenty-one and a half, it was a great adventure and everyone had fully believed it would be over in a matter of months.

It was a strange feeling when, with every step, I was reminiscing back to December 1939, when we were free.

Now, I was by myself, with a mixture of hatred and joy in my system, and at that time of the morning, everything was so quiet, with not a soul to be seen. This was quite lucky as it allowed me to recapture my thoughts and feelings and compose myself before arriving home.

I arrived at the house, walked to the front door and raised the knocker. I knew that Doreen would be in bed and my father still at work, and although they had received a telegram saying that I was safe and well and had landed in this country, they did not know exactly when I would arrive home. This was on Friday, 25th April 1945, at 7. 30 in the morning, and I had only been liberated on 21st April 1945.

Doreen was rather surprised to see me standing outside, and in no time at all, she had me sitting down to a hearty breakfast. It was a bit upsetting to see my mother's usual place at the table occupied by Doreen, but I managed to get over that hurdle. I explained to Doreen that I now held a double ration book for the next eight weeks, which was granted to all returning Prisoners of War.

In less than one hour my father would be returning home from work, therefore, we spoke about many of the local happenings of the last five years and, more especially, of my mother's death, although Doreen had been very good and had filled me in well with a lot of the details in all her letters that I had received at the camps.

At around 8.15am, I heard my father arriving at the back door, and I went to meet him. He, too, was astonished at seeing me. Within a very short time of this, the news got around to the neighbours of my arrival home, and so we had a constant stream of visitors of all ages. One thing that sticks in my mind was a senior husband and his wife, who lived opposite and were good friends of my parents. They had always spoken in Welsh to me, from a very early age. Naturally, the welcome was all in Welsh, and I was so tongue-tied that I replied in Polish and German, as I had not spoken my native language for so long, which caused a big laugh between us all.

Needless to say, the welcome from all the neighbours and friends was great and many of them brought gifts of food with them, spared from their weekly rations, which I understood had been pretty tight in the latter years. People kept calling throughout the next few days, but I did manage one short walk to Cwmaman post office, to send a telegram of my homecoming to my aunt and uncle, who lived in Penegoes, Machynlleth, a journey that normally took ten minutes but took hours, due to meeting various friends and neighbours. I also could not shake hands with them, due to my hands still being bandaged because of the frostbite.

On Sunday morning, I felt it was my duty to attend the Baptist chapel for the morning service. I had done this regularly until 1938, when I was transferred to Oliver's footwear in Haverfordwest. Although not a Baptist member, along with my two friends, I regularly attended the chapel three times every Sunday, but it had been my mother's wish that I remained a Wesleyan. Discreetly entering the chapel after the service had started, I sat in one of the back pews, where I had always sat with the boys, but on this occasion, I was on my own as the rest of my friends had not returned. Half way through the service, the minister announced from the pulpit that there was a member in the congregation who had returned from captivity, and he used this as his theme for the children's story. This shattered my belief that I had sneaked into the back pew completely unnoticed. After the service, I was again warmly welcomed home.

Arriving home later, it felt strange to sit down to Sunday lunch with just my father and Doreen, and in the evening, I accompanied Doreen to the Wesleyan chapel, for the evening service, where I had been a member since 1936. Doreen was the organist and so she left me to sit and reminisce in my mother's pew. Although I was known to most of the congregation, I was a stranger to the new minister, who had attended my mother's funeral. Again, I was welcomed like I had been at the Baptist service in the morning, and I nervously stood up and thanked everyone for their welcome.

As the days went on, I was told that two other boys, both members of the Baptist chapel, were due home from Prisoner of War camps.

I had heard from my aunt and uncle in Machynlleth, urging me to visit them as soon as possible, so, just a few days later, I decided to travel up by train. I was again overwhelmed by the welcome I received from my aunt, friends and neighbours. I was given lots of gifts from the village where I had spent my childhood. It was such a treat to see fresh eggs, meat and butter, which were not available in Aberdare with the weekly rations. I had only been there a couple of days, when I received a letter informing me that I had to attend a medical board in Cardiff.

It was now essential that I returned to Cardiff for the medical board. Still being in uniform, I was able to travel at reduced fare. By this time, the six month's leave I had been given was slowly ebbing away. Food was more plentiful with my aunt in Machynlleth, and they wanted me to go back there after the board, for a few more days, to continue to build me up.

At the end of my six month's leave, I was informed that I was to travel to Morpeth, Newcastle-upon-Tyne, for a six-week induction course, and after I had completed this course, I went to my regiment at Sandown, to join the training battalion at Sandown Park, in Esher, Surrey, towards the end of July 1945. After approximately four months at Sandown, I rejoined the battalion until early November 1945, when the whole of the third battalion were moved by rail to Selkirk, in Scotland, then, in a matter of days, the whole battalion were moved again back to Aylesbury, before being sent home for seven days Christmas leave.

On Christmas night, I was hoping to attend the local welfare dance hall in Aberaman, but not only did I fail to get in as it was packed, the weather was atrocious (a very stormy night) and, unfortunately, none of my mates were home on leave. I was therefore very pleased to return to Esher and enjoy the local festivities.

On returning to Sandown Park, we were told to join the Third Battalion stationed at Great Missenden, to wait for our demob, but this was not a good place to be sent, as there was quite a big distance between the railway station and the camp.

I was suffering from toothache from some broken teeth, so I was obliged to visit the camp dentist for a session, and he decided I needed to be fitted with a small plate and two or three false teeth. The work on this was to be completed when I arrived at the next camp, which was Caerphilly, in Wales. We arrived at Caerphilly and had to wait for the final demobilisation date, which was to be just a few days later. We were given our demob papers and then we were taken to Hereford, to receive our civilian suit and other things. My final step in the army was to finally finish in January 1946, after nearly five years, with six weeks paid leave.

When I got home, I decided to apply to my old employer, George Oliver Footwear Ltd., and I was invited to attend an interview in Cardiff. I was given a job and told to report to the Newport branch in the High Street, the following week.

I remained with Oliver's until my retirement from the Aberystwyth branch in April 1983, after forty-five years in total with the company.